11 $\frac{95}{}$

KHANIQAHI NIMATULLAHI
(SUFI ORDER)

306 West 11th Street
New York, NY, 10014 -USA
Tel: 212 924.7739
Fax: 212 924.5479

4931 MacArthur Blvd. NW
Washington, DC 20007 -USA
Tel: 202-338.4757

84 Pembroke Street
Boston, MA 02118 -USA
Tel: 617-536.0076

4642 North Hermitage
Chicago, IL 60640 -USA
Tel: 312-561.1616

4021 19th Avenue
San Francisco, CA 94132 -USA
Tel: 415-586.1313

11019 Arleta Avenue
Mission Hills,
Los Angeles, CA 91345 -USA
Tel: 818-365.2226

219 Chace Street
Santa Cruz, CA 95060 -USA
Tel: 408-425.8454

405 Greg Avenue
Santa Fe, NM 87501 -USA
Tel: 505-983.8500

310 NE 57th Street
Seattle, WA 98105 -USA
Tel: 206-527.5018

41 Chepstow Place
London W2 4TS
England
Tel: 071-229-0769

The Old Windmill, Sulgrave,
Banbury, Oxfordshire
OX17 2SH England
Tel: 0295-760.361

95 Old Lansdowne Rd.
West Disdbury, Manchester,
M20 8NZ, England
Tel: 061-434.8857

Kölnerstraße 176
5000 Köln 90 (Porz)
Germany
Tel: 49-2203.15390

Van Blankenburgstraat 66B
2517 XS 's-Gravenhage,
The Netherlands
Tel: 070-345.0251

50 Rue du 4ème Zouaves
Rosny-sous-Bois 93110,
Paris, France
Tel: 48-552.809

Viale Liberazione, 1
Vaiano Cremasco (CR)
Milan, Italy
Tel: 39-373.277.246

63 Boulevard Latrille
BP 1224 Abidjan
CIDEX 1 Côte d'Ivoire
Africa
Tel: 225-410.510

87A Mullen Street
Balmain, 2041
Sydney, Australia
Tel: 612-555.7546

SUFISM II

KHANIQAHI NIMATULLAHI
(SUFI ORDER)

Also available by Dr. Javad Nurbakhsh

SUFISM II

Fear and Hope

Contraction and Expansion

Gathering and Dispersion

Intoxication and Sobriety

Annihilation and Subsistence

Dr. Javad Nurbakhsh

KHANIQAHI-NIMATULLAHI PUBLICATIONS
LONDON & NEW YORK

Translated by William C. Chittick
Cover Design by Alex Cowie

Second printing 1993

ISBN 09-933546-07-6

Printed in the United States of America on Acid Free Paper

Published by Khaniqahi-Nimatullahi Publications (KNP)
306 W. 11th Street
New York, New York 10014 -USA
Telephone: (212) 924-7739
Facsimile: (212) 924-5479

CONTENTS

IN HIS NAME

Sufism is a reality of many dimensions, touching every facet of human existence. Over the centuries, the masters of the Path have composed works dealing with all the different aspects of Sufi teaching and practice. They have discussed the nature of the Divine Being, often in terms of His Attributes and how these become manifest in His Acts (that is, in all the myriad forms of created existence). Basing themselves on the *Koran* and the *Ahadith* (or sayings of the Prophet) and aided by their own direct visions of the Truth—their "unveilings," they have written innumerable works, from lengthy tomes to brief poems, setting forth the nature of reality. Having prayed to God in the manner of the Prophet, "Oh God, show us all things as they truly are," and having received the answer to their prayers, they have attempted to express their ineffable visions in words.

In contrast with works dealing mainly with Sufi teachings about the nature of things, many other works were composed to explain the details of Sufi practice—all the modes of "remembering" God and of delivering the mind and the heart from the veil of "others".

Still another category of Sufi literature deals with the inward transformations and transmutations that the travelers undergo on the way to God. In the classical terminology of Sufism, these spiritual experiences are summarized under the heading of the "stations" *(maqāmāt)* and the "states" *(ahvāl)*. In the present volume, we have gathered together the writings of a number of great Sufi masters concerning ten of these stations and states that are usually discussed in pairs. These writings contain important teachings that every Sufi should have knowledge of so that he may compare his own inward experiences with those described by the masters and thus not fall into error in the perception of his own situation.

Dr Javad Nurbakhsh

Fear and Hope

The gentleness of union has gone,
clear out of mind.
We have been left burning
in fear and hope.

'Attār

FEAR

Fear (*khawf*) signifies a feeling of impending danger. It has been defined as "pain and burning in the heart because of the expectation of something unpleasant in the future."

Certain authorities have written that fear is a state pertaining only to those Sufis who are beginners on the Path. However, if we accept the principle that from the first step the Sufi takes upon the way he must live in the present and forget both past and future, we must say that the Sufi has no fear. Rather, fear is the state of a person who is seeking the path of God and has repented but has not yet become a Sufi. "Surely God's friends—no fear shall be on them, neither shall they sorrow" (*Koran,* X:63).

THE KINDS OF FEAR

Those who have fear in the path of religion have been divided into six categories as follows: (1) believers

1

(*mo'men*) have fear (*khawf*), (2) worshippers (*'abed*) have fright (*vajal*), (3) ascetics (*zāhed*) have dread (*rahbat*), (4) knowers of the religion (*'alem*) have apprehension (*kheshyat*), (5) knowers of God (*'āref*) have solicitude (*eshfāq*), and (6) truthful servants (*seddiq*) have awe (*haybat*).

1. Abu 'Ali Daqqāq says, "Fear is a precondition and a characteristic of faith. God says, 'Fear me, if you have faith' (*Koran*, III:175)." (*Resāla-ye qoshayriyah*)

2. God says, "Their hearts frightened . . ." (*Koran*, XXIII:60). Fright is stronger than fear; it is a fear pertaining to those whose hearts are alive. It has three aspects: fear for obedience, fear for the present moment, and fear toward expectations. The servant's fear for obedience derives from three things: corruption of his intention, punishment for failings, and retribution of enemies. Fear for the present moment derives from a change in one's resolution, restlessness of the mind, and dispersion in the heart. Finally, fear toward expectations derives from the remembrance of what must not be done (which occurs to the extent of one's unveiling and the vision of one's heart) and from worry over what has passed. Keeping one's eye upon the Beginning maintains the heart in its restlessness and drowns its desires. This is the fear of worshippers. (Adapted from Ansāri, *Sad maydān*)

3. God says, "Have dread of Me" (*Koran*, II:40). Dread is a fear beyond fright and has three attributes: it takes away enjoyment, cuts the servant off from the creatures and the world, and within the world separates him from the world. Dread also has three signs: its possessor sees his own ego as his punishment, his words as all complaints, and his acts as all sins. He sees himself constantly charging and burning among three states: the affliction of the diseased,

2

the sincerity of the drowned, and the supplication of the humble supplicators. This is the fear of the ascetics. (*Ibid.*)

4. Daqqāq says, "Apprehension is acquired through knowledge (*'elm*). God says, 'Only those of His servants who have knowledge are apprehensive of God' (*Koran,* XXXV:28)." (*Resāla-ye qoshayriyah*)

5. God says, "Those who are solicitous in apprehension of their Lord . . ." (*Koran,* XXIII:57). Solicitude is continual fear; it is a cloud raining down light. This fear places no veil before fervent prayer, no covering over insight, no wall before hope; it melts away and attracts. Until the servant hears the good news—"Fear not, nor have sorrow!" (*Koran,* XLI:30)—he gains no rest. God bestows solicitude upon him in generosity and keeps him burning in worry over its disappearance. He increases his light, and He throws anxiety into him over its being taken away. In his alienation, God pulls him up, while He throws rebuke into his heart. This fear is that of the knowers of God. (Adapted from Ansāri, *Sad maydān*)

6. Daqqāq says, "Awe is a precondition of knowledge of God. As God says, 'God warns you to be beware of Him' (*Koran,* III:28)." (*Resāla-ye qoshayriyah*). The fear of the elect resides in their awe of Majesty, not in their fear of chastisement. Fear of chastisement is to worry for oneself and one's welfare, but awe of Majesty is reverence for God and forgetfulness of self.

God says, "He knows what is within your selves, so beware of Him!" (*Koran,* II:235). Awe is the station of the purified and the degree of the saints. Awe is a fear that is born only from direct vision, while other fears may derive from transmitted sayings. Awe is a bewilderment that flashes in the heart like lightning; if the breeze of intimacy does not blow in the face of it, a man's soul will not be able to bear it and will usually fall into a state of ecstasy, just as Moses fell into such a state at Mt. Sinai (*Koran,* VII:143). Awe does not occur from the threat of chastisement but from awareness. It opens the way for three things: joy in the present moment, being lost to oneself, and becoming naughted from self-will and worldly desires. The awe that derives from insight gives birth to wisdom; that which derives from meditation gives birth to discernment; and that which derives from music (*samā‘*) either kills or takes away the intellect and senses. (Ansāri, *Sad maydān*)

Abol-Qāsem Hakim says, "Fear is of two kinds: dread and apprehension. When the possessor of dread has fear, he seeks refuge in flight, but the possessor of apprehension seeks refuge in God." (*Resāla-ye qoshayriyah*)

'Ezzod-Din Kāshānī says, "Fear is an attribute of those who are veiled. In the state of contemplation, it is obliterated. But apprehension and awe are the attributes of the people of unveilings, contemplations, and direct visions; through them they are protected from the blows of might they would suffer from audacity and story-telling." (*Mesbāh al-hedāyah*)

Depending on its object, fear can be ascribed in different ways to different groups of people: (1) The ascetic fears going to hell, (2) The knower of God fears distance from Him, (3) The sage (*hakim*) fears going astray, (4) The knower of the religion ("clergyman," *ʿālem-e din*) fears committing sins, and (5) The beginning Sufi fears disobeying God.

Finally, we should remind the reader that fear may become a disease, with which a member of any of the above groups may be afflicted.

FEAR AND SORROW, FEAR AND DESPAIR

Whereas sorrow (*hozn*) is related to what has passed, fear pertains to what has not yet come. Despair (*ya's*), on the other hand, is a lack of hope toward the future. He who has despair abandons worship, but he who is overcome by fear goes to extremes in accomplishing his religious acts, to the extent that he harms both himself and those around him.

EXCESSIVE FEAR

Those who have more fear than normal should pay attention to the following points:

1. In the *Koran* God says, "Say: 'O my people who have been immoderate against your own selves! Do not despair of God's mercy! Surely God forgives all sins.'" (*Koran*, XXXIX:53)

2. 'Ali says, "When a servant commits a sin that God covers over in this world, God is too generous to remove its covering in the next world. And when the servant commits a sin for which he is punished in this world, God is too just to punish him again for it in the next world." (*Ehyā' 'olum ad-din*)

3. Jonayd says, "If a single fountainhead of God's generosity were to appear, the evil-doers would be joined to the good-doers." (*Ibid.*)

4. It is said that an unbeliever wanted to be Abraham's guest. Abraham said to him, "If you submit yourself to God, I will accept you as my guest." The unbeliever went away. God then sent Abraham a revelation: "Oh Abra-

ham! You will not give this man dinner until he leaves his own religion! We have been giving him his provisions for seventy years in spite of his unbelief. If you had given him dinner tonight and not attacked him, how would you have lost anything?"

After this revelation, Abraham sought out the unbeliever, brought him back, and gave him dinner. The man then asked him why he had done so. When Abraham related what had happened, the unbeliever said, "If your God is so generous to me, then accept me into your religion!" (*Resāla-ye qoshayriyah*)

5. Mālek ebn Dinār was seen in a dream and asked, "What did God do with you?" He replied, "I met God with many sins, but my good opinion of Him obliterated all of them." (*Ibid.*)

Finally, it should be pointed out that although fear is often mentioned in the *Koran,* the sayings of the Prophet, and the words of the masters of the Path, it is better for us to understand it as referring to the fear of disobeying God and of remaining far from Him. We should realize that God is absolute Good and nothing but Good, and therefore there is no place for fear of Him.

A SAYING OF THE PROPHET CONCERNING FEAR

The Prophet of God has said, "When a man fears God, God makes all things fear Him; but when he does not fear God, God makes him fear all things." (Solami, *Tabaqāt as-sufiyah*)

6

SAYINGS OF THE MASTERS OF THE PATH CONCERNING FEAR

1. He who has fear is he who fears his own self more than Satan. (Abu 'Amr Demashqi, *Ehyā' 'olum ad-din*)

2. Perfect faith is attained through knowledge (*'elm*), and perfect knowledge is attained through fear. (Sahl Tostari, *'Avāref al-ma'āref*)

3. If it is said to you, "Do you fear God?", and you say "No", you are an unbeliever. But if you say "Yes", you are a liar, for your attributes are not those of someone who fears Him. (Fozayl ebn 'Eyāz, *Ibid.*)

4. When certainty is soundly established within the heart, so too is fear. (Dhon-Nun, *Tabaqāt as-sufiyah*)

5. When fear takes up residence in the heart, sensual desires are burned away and forgetfulness is thrown out. (Abu Solaymān Dārāni, *Tabaqāt as-sufiyah;* in *Resāla-ye qoshayriyah* attributed to Ebrāhim Shaybān)

6. Everything has a mark of sincerity, and the mark of certainty's sincerity is fear of God. (Abu Solaymān Dārāni, *Tabaqāt as-sufiyah*)

7. To the extent that you love God, the creatures will love you. To the extent that you fear God, the creatures will have awe of you. And to the extent that you occupy yourself with God, the creatures will occupy themselves with your tasks. (Yahyā ebn Ma'ādh, *Ibid.*)

8. God created hearts as the abode of remembrance, but they became the abode of sensual desires. Nothing obliterates those desires from the heart except unsettled fear or

7

disquieted yearning. ('Abdollāh ebn Khobayq, *Tabaqāt as-sufiyah*)

9. The most profitable fear is that which holds you back from acts of disobedience, prolongs your sorrow over what you have missed, and makes you think about the remainder of your life. (*Ibid.*)

10. Fear of God will take you to God; pride and self-satisfaction will cut you off from God, and disdain for people in your soul is a tremendous disease that cannot be remedied. (Abu 'Othmān Hiri, *Ibid.*)

11. Know that knowledge is a leader, fear a driver, and the ego obstinate between the two. It is recalcitrant, deceptive, and sly. So beware of it, watch over it with the discipline of knowledge, and drive it with the threats of fear. Then will you accomplish what you desire. ('Amr ebn 'Omar, *Ibid.*)

12. The fruit of gratitude is love for God and fear of Him. (Mohammad ebn Fazl Balkhi, *Ibid.*)

13. The mark of the saints is that they fear being cut off from God because of the intensity of their preference and yearning for Him in their hearts. (Mohammad ebn 'Al-iyān, *Ibid.*)

14. Fear is the restlessness of hearts due to their knowledge of the violent Power of the Object of their worship. (Mohammad ebn Khafif, *Resāla-ye qoshayriyah*)

15. Fear is God's whip through which He rectifies fugitives from His gate. (Abu Hafs, *Ibid.*)

16. Fear is the heart's lamp through which is seen the good and evil within it. (*Ibid.*)

17. Fear is that you do not distract yourself with "maybe" and "some day". (Abu 'Ali Daqqāq, *Ibid.*)

18. He who has fear is he who has gained security from frightful things. (Ebn Jalā', *Ibid.*)

19. He who has fear is not he who weeps and wipes his eyes, but he who abandons that thing for which he fears he may be chastised. (*Resāla-ye qoshayriyah*)

20. Fozayl ebn 'Eyāz was asked, "How is it that we see no fearful men?" He replied, "If you had fear, you would see the fearful. He who has fear sees none but the fearful. The mother bereaved of her child prefers to see bereaved mothers like herself." (*Ibid.*)

21. Poor son of Adam! If he feared the Fire the way he fears poverty, he would enter paradise. (Yahyā ebn Ma'ādh, *Ibid.*)

22. The sign of fear is constant sorrow. (Shāh Shojā' Kermāni, *Ibid.*)

23. He who fears something flees from it, but he who fears God flees toward Him. (Abol-Qāsem Hakim, *Ibid.*)

24. Dhon-Nun was asked, "When does the way of fear become easy for the servant?" He answered, "When he considers himself ill and avoids all things for fear of prolonging his illness." (*Resāla-ye qoshayriyah*)

25. Fear of God is an angel that takes up residence only in a pious heart. (Beshr Hāfi, *Ibid.*)

26. A fearful man is imperfect in his fear when he remains calm in the face of it—for it is subtle and hidden. (Abu 'Othmān Hiri, *Ibid.*)

27. He who has fear flees from his Lord to his Lord. (Nuri, *Ibid.*)

28. The mark of fear is bewilderment and halting at the gate to the Unseen. (*Resāla-ye qoshayriyah*)

29. Fear is the expectation of punishment with every breath. (Jonayd, *Ibid.*)

30. Fear never leaves a heart without that heart being ruined. (Abu Solaymān Dārāni, *Ibid.*)

31. The sincerity of fear lies in abstinence from sins outwardly and inwardly. (Abu 'Othmān Hiri, *Ibid.*)

32. Men remain upon the way as long as they have fear. When fear leaves them, they go astray. (Dhon-Nun, *Ibid.*)

33. Everything has an adornment. The adornment of worship is fear, and the mark of fear is paucity of expectations. (Hātem Asamm, *Ibid.*)

34. Fear is firm knowledge concerning the course of God's decrees. (*Resāla-ye qoshayriyah*)

35. Fear is the heart's movement and agitation due to God's Majesty. (*Ibid.*)

36. The heart must not let anything overcome it except fear, for if hope should overcome it, it will become corrupted. O disciple! Through fear the travelers ascend; but if they should lose it, then they will descend. (Abu Solaymān Dārāni, *Ibid.*)

FURTHER WORDS OF THE MASTERS CONCERNING FEAR

Fear is the fortress of faith, the sovereign remedy of piety, and the weapon of the believer. It is of three kinds: transitory, permanent, and overpowering.

Transitory fear enters the heart and then passes on. It is the least of fears. If not for it, there would be no faith, for without fear, there is no trace of security, and without security, no faith. The marks of fear are hidden, but it is the ornament of faith. A man has just as much faith as he has fear.

Permanent fear holds the servant back from acts of disobedience. It keeps him away from forbidden things and shortens his expectations.

Overpowering fear is the fear of deception. Through it the Truth can be attained; it opens the way toward sincerity and holds a man back from forgetfulness. There are ten signs of deception: (1) obedience without the taste of sweetness, (2) perseverance without repentence, (3) shutting the door of supplication, (4) theory without practice, (5) wisdom without resolution, (6) companionship without reverence, (7) closing the door of humble entreaty, (8) companionship with bad men, and, worse than all else, (9) that God should give the servant faith without certainty and, (10) that God should leave the servant to his own devices. This kind of fear is the fear of those who repent. (Ansāri, *Sad maydān*)

* * *

Fear is of two kinds: fear of punishment and fear of deception. Fear of punishment belongs to the common believers. It has two causes: belief in God's threats and awareness of one's own sins. It has two signs: avoiding the commission of sins in the future and hurrying to make up for sins committed in the past. The heat of this fear can be dampened by taking into account God's promises giving hope. For example, it has been related that He said, "There are two fears and two securities that I do not combine in My servant. When someone fears Me in this world, I give him security on the Day of Resurrection. But when someone feels secure from Me in this world, I make him fear the Day of Resurrection."

Although the person who fears punishment has faith in the Unseen, he is not one of the People of Love for he fears the punishment of his own self, proving that he loves himself. But no one whose heart has love for himself loves God, since wherever the sultan of God's Love takes up residence, it leaves no room for any other boarder.

As for the fear of deception, it pertains to the lovers of God's attributes. They are attached to the Attributes of Beauty, such as Kindness, Mercy, Gentleness and Good-pleasure; and they fear and avoid the Attributes of Majesty, such as Punishment, Severity and Wrath. In the face of His apparent Gentleness, they have no security from hidden Severity. They constantly fear an evil end and the call of the cutting of bonds.

As for the saying of the Prophet, "The beginning of wisdom is the fear of God," it is exemplified by the wise man who, out of prudence, never rests in the face of an anticipated deception and is never deceived by the well-being of his present state. How could a prudent man be secure from being surprised by the Divine Wrath? Verily, the eternal Attributes are not the result of the servant's acts.

The causes of the fear of deception are two-fold: love for God and the observation of deception. Its signs are also two-fold. First, everyone fears its possessor, since his fear is accompanied by a trace of the divine Majesty and Awesomeness. In the words of the Prophet, "When a man fears God, all things fear him." Second, he fears nothing but God. As has been said, "The fearful man fears only

God." The following story has been related by Sahl ebn
'Abdollāh:

> One day I was walking in the desert. I saw a man
> and conceived a fear of him. I said to him, "Are you a
> jinn or a man? You have caused me to fear."
> He replied, "Are you a believer or an unbeliever?
> For you have thrown me into doubt."
> I answered, "A believer."
> He said, "Be silent, for the believer fears none
> but God."

Fear of God is in truth this fear of deception, not the
fear of punishment. Fear of deception is the result of love
for God and the glorification of Him. But fear of punishment is the result of love for the self and solicitude for it.
Nevertheless, although fear of deception results from love
of God, it is marred by seeking the enjoyment of proximity and the craving for union. The arena of Love, however, is free of all causes.

Although in the end no fear remains for advanced
Sufis, in the rawness of their original state and until they
become "cooked," travelers have no escape from fear's
heat. Thus Dhon-Nun says, "The lover will not be given
the cup of love to drink from until fear cooks his heart."
This occurs in the following way. First, the heart of the
traveler falls into the narrow confines of the fear of
punishment, and from the glow of that heat it becomes
half-cooked. Part of the rawness of craving for the objects
of his desire and the darkness of seeking pleasures leaves
him, so the veil covering him becomes thin. From beyond
this thin veil, the light of the Attributes' beauty begins to
shine and its reflection falls into his eye. Then, love for the
Attributes' beauty appears within him, fear of punishment
packs its bags and leaves, and the fear of deception arrives. His half-cooked heart falls into the heat of this fear

13

and finally becomes completely cooked. The remainder of the rawness of craving and the darkness of seeking pleasures is totally left behind him while he remains within the narrow confines of this fear. Absolute purity makes its appearance, and that thin veil also disappears. The brilliance of the light of the Essence makes contact with the heart, and the hand of Generosity clothes him in the robe of love for that Essence. Then he throws off the covering of luminous and dark existence, just as he has passed beyond the pleasures of the self and the heart through the first and second cooking. He shakes the skirt of his aspiration free of any attention toward his own existence. Finally, union and separation, proximity and distance, are all the same in his eyes. In this station, the term "friendship" is truly applied to the individual, and sorrow along with fear is lifted from him—for God's friends have neither sorrow nor fear: "Surely God's friends—no fear shall be on them, neither shall they sorrow" (*Koran,* X:63). ('Ezzod-Din Kāshāni, *Mesbāh al-hedāyah*)

HOPE

> *Hast Thou entered from the door of peace,*
> *or that of war?*
> *Should I walk with the foot of fear,*
> *or that of hope?*
>
> *Sa'di*

Hope (*rajā'*) signifies the expectation of something desired. It is higher than fear. The beginning Sufi spends most of his time in hope, since God's nearest servant is he who loves Him most, and love is accompanied by hope. In the *Koran* God says, "And those who emigrate and struggle in God's way—those have hope in God's mercy" (*Koran,* II:218).

It is said that a bedouin once came before the Prophet of God and asked, "Who will settle the accounts of the creatures?"

The Prophet answered, "God Almighty."

The bedouin asked, "All alone?"

The Prophet replied in the affirmative. Then the bedouin smiled. The Prophet said, "O bedouin, why are you smiling?"

He answered, "When a generous person evaluates someone, he pardons him; and when he settles accounts with him, he treats him with indulgence."

FURTHER INQUIRY INTO THE NATURE OF HOPE

Every thought of good and evil that passes through a person's heart is related to the past, the present, or the future. If it is related to the past, it is called "remembrance" or "recollection." If it is related to the present, it is called "sensation", "intuition" or "perception." And if it is related to the future, it is called "expectation" or "anticipation".

If the object of expectation is unpleasant and results in the heart's suffering, the expectation is called "fear". However, if it is something desirable and produces happiness in the heart, the expectation is called "hope." What you expect must have a cause. If you expect it because most of the causes are at hand, then it is correct to refer to "hope". But if its causes are not to be found, then the expectation can better be referred to as "foolishness" or "stupidity." If its causes are neither known nor determined, then that expectation is best called a "wish" since there is no reason for it.

The difference between wishing and hoping is that the person who wishes , unlike one who has hope, is inactive and does not enter into the path of earnestness and effort. That is, hope results in effort, while wishful thinking is defective.

'Ezzod-Din Kāshāni writes, "He who has hope in something but does not hasten to perform the acts that will lead to its attainment is called a 'wisher' or a 'pretender,' not a man of hope." (*Mesbāh al-hedāyah*)

THE KINDS OF HOPE

Ascetics hope for heaven and its rewards. Knowers of the religion hope that God will forgive them their sins. Beginning Sufis hope that God will ignore their slips and bring them closer to Himself. Knowers of God hope that they will attain the vision of God and that God will not keep them in separation. Sages hope that in the expanse of His mercy God will forgive them.

Abu Nasr Sarrāj writes, "Hope is of three kinds: hope in God, hope in the expanse of God's mercy, and hope in God's reward." (*al-Loma'*)

DEFINITIONS OF HOPE BY THE MASTERS OF THE PATH

1. The mark of hope is excellent obedience. (Shāh Shojā', *Ehyā'* and *Resāla-ye qoshayriyah*)

2. Hope is to see Majesty with the eye of Beauty. (*Ehyā'* and *Resāla-ye qoshayriyah*)

3. Hope is refreshment of the heart through the vision of ₍the generosity of the Object of hope, the Beloved. (Abu 'Abdollāh ebn Khafif, *'Avāref al-ma'āref* and *Resāla-ye qoshayriyah*)

4. Hope is desire for God's Bounty and Mercy and main-

taining the sincerity of one's good opinion of Him at the arrival of death. (Hāreth Mohāsebi, *Tabaqāt as-sufiyah*)

5. Sincerity is known through perseverance, perseverance through hope, hope through will, and will through knowledge of God. (Hātem Asamm, *Ibid.*)

6. Hope is of three kinds: first, a man performs a good work and hopes for its acceptance. Second, a man performs a bad work, then repents and hopes for forgiveness. Third, a man is a liar; he persists in sins, and then he says, "I hope for forgiveness." But he who knows himself to be an evildoer must have greater fear than hope. (Ebn Khobayq, *Resāla-ye qoshayriyah*)

7. Hope is confidence in the bestowal of the Generous and Loving God. (*Resāla-ye qoshayriyah*)

8. Hope is the heart's proximity to God's Kindness. (*Ibid.*)

9. Hope is the heart's joy in the wonderful place to which it will return. (*Ibid.*)

10. Hope is vision of the wide expanse of God's Mercy. (*Ibid.*)

11. The mark of hope in the servant is that when he is encompassed by God's good-doing, his heart fills with gratitude, hoping that God will complete His bounty upon him in this world and pardon him totally in the next world. (Ahmad ebn 'Āsem Antāki, *Ibid.*)

12. Hope is to rejoice at the existence of His Bounty. (Abu 'Abdollāh ebn Khafif, *Ibid.*)

13. My hope in Thee in spite of my sins almost outweighs my hope in Thee because of my works. For in my works I

find myself depending upon my own sincerity, but how can I guard my works, since I am known for my imperfections? But in my sins I find myself depending upon Thy pardon, and how shouldst Thou not pardon them, since Thou art described by Generosity? (Yahyā ebn Ma'ādh, *Ibid.*)

14. My God, the most delightful of Thy gifts in my heart is hope in Thee; the sweetest words upon my tongue are Thy praise, and the dearest of my hours are the hours wherein I gaze upon Thee. (*Ibid.*)

15. Hope is that you hope He does not cut you off with less than Himself. (Shebli, *al-Loma'*)

FURTHER WORDS OF THE MASTERS CONCERNING HOPE

God says, "Being afraid of the world to come and hoping for the mercy of his Lord . . ." (*Koran,* XXXIX:9). Certainty has two wings: fear and hope. Who can fly with only one wing?

Hope provides the mount for service, the provisions for effort, and the supplies for worship. Faith is like a balance: on one pan is fear and on the other hope. The fulcrum is love, and the pans are hung from the virtues.

> *The bird of faith has two wings:*
> *fear and hope.*
> *How can you make your bird fly*
> *without wings?*

Hope is of three kinds:

First is the hope of the wrongdoers that God will forgive their sins and accept once again His enemies.

18

"They hope for His mercy and fear His chastisement" (*Koran*, XVII:57).

Second is the hope of those who follow a middle course that God will forgive their defects, accept their obedience, and increase His aid towards them. "They hope for a commerce that comes not to naught" (*Koran*, XXXV:29).

Third is the hope of those who are foremost in God's way that He will complete His eternal bounty toward them, increase the life of their hearts, and preserve their hearts and the substance of the present moment. "You are hoping from God for that for which they cannot hope" (*Koran*, IV:104). (Ansāri, *Sad maydān*)

* * *

For the common people, hope is the expectation of that which is absent and the seeking of one's desire. However, in the path of God, hope is complaint and blindness. He who strives in the way of His love, who becomes submerged within the sea of ecstasy, and upon whom falls the rain of His Goodness does not ask for anything more than what reaches him and overcomes him from his Lord. He has no other desire in the two worlds. Thus, hope is weakness and limitation. It is a defect in the path of man's primordial nature, commerce instead of servanthood.

The hope of the elect is thirst for the wine within which they are immersed and with which they are intoxicated. (Ansāri, *'Elal al-maqāmāt*).

The station of hope is discussed after that of fear because the refreshment of hope comes after the torment of fear and because hope's coolness is useful after fear's heat. Since hope results in cooling and refreshment, it is related to Beauty; and since fear results in heating and torment, it is related to Majesty. If the sparks of fear's fire did not help to cook the frozen hearts of the indolent with the heat of seeking, they would remain in the raw state of hardness.

And if hope's fan did not refresh the hearts of the fearful, they would be burned away by fear's heat. Therefore, God's Wisdom placed both hope and fear in the heart of the believer so that through their mixture an equilibrium might appear and faith's temperament might become sound.

Hope and fear are like the two feet of the travelers on the Path by means of which they pass over the stages and way-stations. Sometimes with fear's foot they pass by the perilous places of halting and the inactivity of lassitude. And sometimes with hope's foot they escape from the entanglement of the way's despair and hopelessness. There is no security or resting place wherein they can remedy the thirst of seeking, nor any despair of hopelessness that they might be cut off from their yearning for union.

That which Khājah 'Abdollāh Ansāri has written to diminish the value of the station of hope—"Hope is the weakest way-station of the disciple, since in one respect it is an exchange and in another a protest" ('Elal al-maqāmāt)—cannot be applied to all cases. It is possible for hope to stem from a vision of the generosity of the Object of hope, rather than from a vision of one's own works. Hope can only be an "exchange" if it derives from a vision of one's own works. In the same way, a "protest" is only possible in the case of someone who seeks a specific object of desire, not in the case of the one whose hope is derived from the overpowering force of the theophany of the Attribute of Beauty.

In addition, those who hope are divided into two groups: the seekers of enjoyment and the seekers of God. If a man's hope is confined to the attainment of enjoyment in this world or the next, and if he has an aversion to anything opposed to that, then his hope might leave place for a protest. But the hope of the seekers of God to encounter Him is identical with conformity to His desire. There can be no question of protest, for protest is to seek what is opposed to His desire, while seeking the encounter

20

with Him is not opposed to it. As the Prophet has said, "When a man loves the encounter with God, God loves encounter with him." In truth then, Ansāri's words ("The weakest way-station of the disciple") allude only to these limitations since it is not possible for this "exchange" and "protest" to exist among those who have attained guidance and entered the discipline of the Path.

The mark of the sincerity of hope is the preparation of the means of attaining the Object of one's hope. These means are total attentiveness toward Him and cutting off the attachments that act as hindrances. In the *Koran,* the "negation of association" and "righteous works" allude to these two means: "So let he who hopes for the encounter with his Lord work righteousness and not associate anyone with his Lord in worship" (XVIII:111). ('Ezzod-Din Kāshāni, *Mesbāh al-hedāyah*)

CONTRASTING DEFINITIONS OF FEAR AND HOPE BY THE MASTERS OF THE PATH

1. Fear and hope are like a bird's two wings. When they are harmonious, the bird is harmonious and perfect in his flight. (Abu 'Ali Rudbāri, *Ehyā'*)

2. Fear is male and hope female; from the two are born the realities of faith. (Sahl, *Ibid.*)

3. If the believer's hope and fear were put into a balance, they would be equal. (Motarref, *'A vāref al-ma'āref*)

4. Loqmān said to his son, "Have fear of God, a fear which leaves you no security from His deception. Yet hope with greater intensity than you fear."

His son replied, "How can I do that, since I have only one heart?"

Loqmān said, "Do you not know that the believer has

21

two hearts? With one he fears and with the other he hopes." (*'Avāref al-ma'āref*)

5. Fear guards over works and hope intercedes during tribulations. (Dhon-Nun, *Tabaqāt as-sufiyah*)

6. When hope overcomes fear, the present moment is corrupted. (Abu Solaymān Dārāni, *Ibid.*)

7. The well-being of the heart lies in four characteristics: humility before God, poverty toward Him, fear of Him, and hope in Him. (Abu 'Othmān Hiri, *Ibid.*)

8. He succeeds who fears none but God, who has hope in none but Him, and who prefers His Pleasure over his own caprice. (*Ibid.*)

9. The mark of piety is abstinence, the mark of abstinence is halting in doubtful situations, the mark of fear sorrow, the mark of hope excellent obedience, and the mark of asceticism cutting off one's expectations. (Shāh Shojā', *Ibid.*)

10. Three things come about when *tawhid* is established: fear, hope and love. Fear due to one's many sins is increased by a vision of God's threats. Hope in acquiring good is increased by a vision of His promises. And love for the frequency of remembrance is increased by the vision of His Graciousness. Thus, he who has fear is never relieved of flight; he who has hope is never relieved of seeking, and he who has love is never relieved of the remembrance of the Beloved. Fear is an illuminating fire, hope an illuminating light, and love the light of lights. (Abu 'Ali Jawzjāni, *Ibid.*)

11. Hope is the path of the ascetics and fear the way of the courageous. (Abu Mohammad Jorayri, *Ibid.*)

12. Fear and hope are two halters that prevent bad manners. (Abu Bakr Vāseti, *Ibid.*) Qoshayri gives a slightly different version of this saying: Fear and hope are two halters upon the self that prevent it from embarking upon frivolity. (*Resāla-ye qoshayriyah*)

13. Fear is a veil between the servant and God. Fear is despair and hope is desire. If you fear Him you have considered Him a niggard; if you have hope in Him, you have accused Him. (Abu Bakr Vāseti, *Tabaqāt as-sufiyah*)

14. Fear of God is a defect and a veil. If I fear Him, this does not change what He desires to do with me; nor does my hope in Him help me attain what I desire from Him. Thus, the properties of fear and hope are inactive in those who have attained the Truth. But as for those who are involved with formal things and the religious sciences, they must observe *adab. (Hosri, Ibid.)*

15. There are five [sic] things along with which nothing else may dwell in the heart: fear of God alone, hope in God alone, love for God alone, and intimacy with God alone. (Sari, *Ibid.*)

16. When God manifests Himself to the inmost consciousness, no room is left for hope or fear. (Vāseti, *Resāla-ye qoshayriyah*). Qoshayri comments: There is a certain ambiguity in this saying. Its meaning is that when God's witnesses completely overcome the inmost consciousness, no possibility remains for the remembrance of the temporal things. But fear and hope display a certain subsistence of the awareness of the properties of human nature.

17. When someone fears something other than God, the doors of all things are locked toward him and fear takes mastery over him. It veils him with seventy veils, the least of which is doubt. That which imposes upon such servants

the intensity of their fear is thinking about outcomes and their dread of the changing of states. But God says, "There will appear to them from God what they never reckoned with" (*Koran*, XXXIX:47). And He says, "Say: Shall we tell you who will be the greatest losers in their works? Those whose striving goes astray in the present life, while they think they are working good deeds." (*Koran*, XVIII:104-5). How many are they in enviable positions whose state has then been reversed! They have been afflicted by their association with ugly acts, so intimacy was transformed into alienation and presence into absence. (Hallāj, *Resāla-ye qoshayriyah*)

18. He who mounts upon hope will be held back, and he who mounts upon fear will despair. Rather, sometimes this and sometimes that! (Abu 'Othmān Maghrebi, *Ibid.*)

19. God's call is of three kinds: He calls one person with the voice of threats through Tremendousness; such a one falls into fear. He calls another with the voice of promises through Mercy's bounty; such a one falls into hope. And he calls a third with the voice of Gentleness in accordance with expansion; such a one falls into Love.

The servant must move among these three states. The first is a fear that holds him back from disobedience, the second a hope that maintains his obedience, and the third a love that delivers him from himself. (Ansāri, *Manāzel as-sā'erin*)

20. Fear of God is a whip of archangelic power that strikes the "soul inciting to evil" (*Koran*, XII:53) with the lashes of *adab* so that it may gain the *adab* of the prophets at the ontological level of the archangels. It is a fire deriving from Gods' Magnificence that burns away the veils of the natural constitution in the spiritual heart. It brings about the respect and the dignity of the lover.

Fear is a catapult that throws the boulders of tribulation in order that servanthood may melt within the crucible of Love. Fear encourages good works.

When the lover comes out from the prison of servanthood and is released from the bonds of fear, and when the phoenix of his spirit comes from the exile of tribulation to the plain of freedom, then the subtle realities of the Unseen show their faces without the disruption of fear. The lover is refreshed through the beauty of the Unseen. The zephyr of hope blows within the world of the heart; the water of generosity rains down from the clouds of blessings, and the trees of the mysteries of intimacy begin to grow.

When the spring of hope arrives, the winter of fear takes flight. The sun of Love reaches the constellation of Aries, the world of intellect and knowledge are filled with the blossoms of the new spring of hope, and the nightingales whose tongues had been cut out by the scissors of fear sing the melodies of *tawhid* upon the flowering branches of intimacy.

The hopeful man is God's guest, while the fearful man is His doorman. He who travels by the mount of hope will reach the way-station more quickly than he who travels by fear. (Ruzbehān, *'Abhar al-'āsheqin*)

21.   *The ascetic suffers heartache*
            over his final end—
        What will be his state
            on the Day of Reckoning?
        The knowers of God are aware
            of the Beginning—
        They are free of the heartache and the status
            of the End.
        The knower of God once suffered the heartache
            of hope and fear,
        But his knowledge of what came before
            consumed them both.

25

He is a Knower—he has been delivered
from fear and dread.
God's sword has cut off
all that noise and commotion.

(Rumi, Mathnavi)

22. *When you have no more fear*
or hope,
Then you will be delivered from both arrogance
and humble need.

('Attār)

Contraction and Expansion

Contraction (*qabz*) and expansion (*bast*) are two involuntary spiritual states that descend upon the Sufi from God. A particular kind of expansion and contraction pertains to every station on the Path. Some Sufis have written in praise of contraction and others in praise of expansion; each has praised the one or the other according to his own spiritual state.

The Sufi has submitted himself to God, who says, "God contracts and expands" (*Koran*, II:245). Thus, whether He gives contraction or expansion, the Sufi only desires what is desired by his Beloved.

Contraction and expansion follow upon the states of fear and hope. The difference between the two pairs of spiritual states is that fear and hope are connected with something unpleasant or pleasant in the future, while contraction and expansion are connected to what reaches the Sufi's heart at the present moment. The Sufi usually meets with contraction and expansion in the more exalted levels of his spiritual journey. That is why Sufis have said, "Expansion for the knowers of God is like hope for the disciples, while the former's contraction is like the latter's fear." The masters of the Path consider contraction the result of the Divine Majesty and expansion the effect of the Diving Beauty. The present chapter will attempt to clarify these two states in some detail.

Expansion:

> Our mind is happy and joyful
> in desire for the Friend.
> We will not trade the fire of His love
> for mourning.
>
> Shāh Qāsem Anvār

Contraction:

> You say, "Buy the paradise of cheer
> with the heartache of Love."
> We say, keep the cheer,
> for we will not sell our heartache.
>
> Shāh Ne'matollāh

"Contraction" is a constriction and disheartening of the mind and disposition whose coming and going is outside of the traveler's free choice. In other words, contraction is a spiritual influx that bespeaks of God's rebuke, severity, and chastisement for its recipient. Contraction is fear in the present moment, regret is fear for what is past, and dread and caution are fear for what will come in the future.

"Expansion" is a dilation and gladdening of the mind that cannot be achieved through effort. In other words, it is a spiritual influx that shows God's acceptance, gentleness, mercy, and intimacy to its recipient.

The Sufi masters have sometimes been in contraction and sometimes in expansion. It is true that these two states come from God without any choice on our part, but the Sufi's activities and environment in the past and the present have a certain effect upon their exact nature and intensity.

Hojviri writes, " 'Contraction' is the contraction of the

heart in the state of being veiled, while 'expansion' is the expansion of the heart in the state of unveiling" (*Kashf al-mahjub*). However, this is not a full explanation, for there are many who are veiled but because of their submission to God are in a state of expansion. And there are many in union who because of the fear that their proximity will come to an end are in contraction. Such people say:

> *In proximity remains always*
> *the dread of its passing,*
> *But in distance lies nothing*
> *but hope for union.*
> *Jāmi*

The following anecdote will help explain the above point concerning the definition of expansion and contraction. It is said that as long as he was alive, John the Baptist never smiled, while Jesus never wept, for the one was in the state of contraction and the other in expansion. When they met, John said to Jesus. "O Jesus, have you become secure from being cut off from God?" Jesus replied, "O John, have you despaired of God's mercy? Your weeping will not change the eternal decree, nor will my laughter alter His foreordainment." Thus, neither expansion, contraction, effacement, intimacy, obliteration, eradication, helplessness, nor effort can be anything other than that which was predestined and foreordained. (*Kashf al-mahjub*)

Bāyazid says, "The contraction of the heart lies in the expansion of the ego (*nafs*), while the expansion of the heart lies in the ego's contraction" (*Kashf al-mahjub*). Obviously, if this is so, then one must look for the cause of the heart's contraction in the ego's expansion and *vice versa*. Moreover, this explanation suggests that contraction and expansion are within the reach of man's free will and are connected with his behavior towards his own ego. One can also interpret this saying to mean that the contraction

29

and expansion of the ego are voluntary, while the resulting expansion and contraction of the heart are involuntary.

In the course of his journey to God, the Sufi depends upon both his own effort and God's attraction. In keeping with the verse, "He loves them and they love Him" (*Koran*, V:54), the Sufi loves God and goes toward Him; and God desires the Sufi and pulls him toward Himself. Whenever God's attraction exceeds the traveler's effort, a state of expansion results; whenever the Sufi's effort is greater than God's attraction, he undergoes contraction. Support for this interpretation can be found in Rumi's verse:

> *The love of lovers makes their bodies*
> *thin as bowstrings,*
> *But the love of beloveds makes them*
> *happy and plump.* (Mathnavi)

In other words, the love of lovers ("They love Him") afflicts and distresses them, while the love of beloveds ("He loves them") results in joy and well-being.

SOME EXAMPLES OF CONTRACTION AND EXPANSION

In the state of expansion, the Prophet used to say, "I am the lord of Adam's children, without pride." Again he would say, "I am not like you. I spend my time with God— He gives me food and drink." Yet in the state of contraction, he would say, "I do not know what God will do with you and me. Would that Mohammad's Lord had not created Mohammad!" Or he would say, "O people, do not consider me superior to Jonah (who was imprisoned in the whale because of God's wrath)!" (Maybodi, *Tafsir*)

Shebli passed through both of these stations and gave accounts of them in his sayings. In the station of expansion he would say, "Where are the heavens and the earth so that I can lift them up with my eyelashes?!" Or he would say, "At the Resurrection, everyone has an enemy. My enemy will be Adam. I will say to him, 'Why did you block my way so that I remained in your land of clay?' " (*Ibid.*)

WORDS OF THE MASTERS CONCERNING CONTRACTION AND EXPANSION

When contraction comes to you
    O traveler,
It comes for your own well-being—
    do not despair!
For in expansion and joy
    you keep on expending,
But expenditure requires an income
    for stocking provisions.
If it were always the season
    of summer,
The heat of the sun would set upon
    the garden
And burn up its beds
    to their very roots.
That ancient place
    would never be green again.
Although December's face is sour,
    it is kind.
Summer laughs,
    but also burns.
When contraction comes,
    behold expansion within it!
Be fresh and do not throw wrinkles
    upon your brow!
                    Rumi, Mathnavi

Contraction is the beginning of annihilation, while expansion is the beginning of subsistence. When someone

31

is contracted his state is absence, but when he is expanded, his state is presence. He who is contracted is full of sorrow, but he who is in expansion is full of joy. (Ahmad ebn 'Atā' Rudbāri, *Tabaqāt as-sufiyah*)

*   *   *

When the traveler on the path of the Truth passes beyond the station of God's general Love and reaches the beginnings of His special Love, he becomes one of the Possessors of the Heart, a Master of Spiritual States. At this point, the states of expansion and contraction begin to descend into his heart. The Transformer of hearts—exalted is He!—keeps his heart in a constant state of transformation between these two successive and alternating spiritual states. Finally, He contracts him such that not one of his own enjoyments remains and he becomes expanded in His Light. Sometimes He squeezes him tightly in the fist of contraction so that the excesses of his sensual existence trickle out of him, and perhaps those trickles become manifest in the form of tears. And sometimes He releases his reins in the playing field of expansion so that he may observe the ceremonies of servanthood and sincerity. Thus Vāseti says, "He contracts you away from what belongs to yourself and expands you in what belongs to Him." Similarly Nuri says, "He contracts you toward Himself and expands you in Himself."

What is meant by "contraction" is the disappearance of happiness from the heart when the state of joy is held back and contracted away from it; and what is meant by "expansion" is the illumination of the heart through the shining lights of the state of joy. The reason contraction comes about is the appearance of the ego's attributes, which become a veil. As a result, the heart becomes distressed and grieved. The reason for expansion is the removal of the veil (i.e., the ego) from in front of the heart; as a result the heart opens and expands.

One of the attributes of the ego that brings about the greatest veiling of expansion is rebelliousness. Rebelliousness occurs when a spiritual state descends and brings an influx of joy and expansion that gladdens the heart. The ego "listens by stealth" to this influx (cf. *Koran,* XV:18), thereby becoming apprised of that spiritual state. Then, it begins to tremble because of exultation and exhilaration, and as a result a darkness rises up. Like a layer of clouds, it becomes a veil of the light of the spiritual state, and contraction ensues. The way to fend off this bane is as follows: At the time of the descent of the influx of joy, the heart must take refuge in the Divine presence before the ego can listen by stealth; it must turn toward Him in sincerity and devotion, so that He may place a curtain of impeccability between it and the ego to preserve it from the ego's obstinacy and rebelliousness. Jonayd was asked, "Which of your moments do you regret?" He answered, "The time of expansion that results in contraction, or the time of intimacy that results in alienation."

It often happens that beginners find a grief or exultation within themselves which they take for contraction or expansion in the heart, but in this way they are mistaken. Shaykh al-Islām Sohravardi has defined grief and exultation as follows: "Grief is the blazing up of the collar that holds back the dog of the ego, while exultation is the rising of the ego's waves when the ocean of the natural disposition is in tumult."

Since the end of contraction is expansion and the end of expansion is annihilation, and since contraction and expansion cannot occur along with annihilation, Abol-Qāsem Fāres has said, "First contraction appears, then expansion, then there is neither one nor the other."

Contraction and expansion are spiritual states, and therefore beginners have no share in them. Moreover, since the advanced are no longer affected by spiritual states, they have passed beyond them. Hence, these two spiritual states are peculiar to intermediate travelers. In place of contraction and expansion, beginners experience fear and hope and the advanced experience annihilation and subsistence. Because of their faith, both beginners and

33

intermediates possess fear and hope in common, in the same way that, due to their natural dispositions, they share grief and exultation. However, since the advanced have cast off their existence, they possess neither contraction nor expansion, neither fear nor hope, neither grief nor exultation. Since their egos have attained to the station of the heart, they manifest the heart's attributes. Therefore, grief and exultation are transformed into contraction and expansion, and these remain within the ego instead of within the heart. ('Ezzod-Din Kāshāni, *Mesbāh al-hedāyah*)

*   *   *

God says, "Thereafter we contract it to Ourselves, a gentle contraction" (*Koran, XXV:46*). Here "contraction" alludes to the station of "those who are kept back"—those whom God stores away for His own use. Such people may be classified into three groups. God contracts one group to Himself through the contraction of death, and thus He holds them back from the eyes of all creatures. He contracts another group by hiding them within the clothing of disguise; He places over them the garlands of phenomenal existence and conceals them from the world's eyes. A third group, He contracts away from themselves to Himself, shows them His sincere love within their inmost consciousnesses, and keeps them back from themselves. (Ansāri, *Manāzel as-sā'erin*)

*   *   *

God also says, "Therein multiplying you" (*Koran,* XLII:11). Expansion signifies that the outward appearances of the servant are placed within the ascending degrees of knowledge, while the cloak of special regard is draped over his inward reality. These are the People of Disguise. They are expanded within the field of expansion for one of three reasons, to each of which pertains a particular group:

One group are expanded as a mercy to the creatures.

This group expound for the creatures and mingle with them that they may derive illumination from their light. At the same time, their realities remain gathered and the inmost secrets safeguarded.

A second group are expanded because of the strength of their inward realities and the determination of their viewpoints, for they are a group whose object of vision is not disturbed by outward appearances, nor is their object of contemplation moved by the winds of phenomenal existence, for they are expanded within the fist of contraction.

A third group are expanded as signposts on the Way, as leaders of guidance and lamps for the travelers. (*Ibid.*)

*　　*　　*

The eighty-fifth battlefield is expansion, which is born from the battlefield of riches. God says, "Is he whose breast God has dilated for Islam, so that he walks in a light from his Lord [no better than one who is hard-hearted] . . .?" (*Koran*, XXXIX:22). Expansion signifies that God has dilated the servant's heart, his spiritual moment, and his aspiration. It too is of three kinds: expansion in supplication, in service, and in seeking.

Expansion in supplication has three signs: intimate whispering with God together with reverence, humility together with awe, and prayer for the good. Expansion in service also has three signs: abundant tasks performed with ease, abundant litanies (*verd*) recited in concealment from people, and the heart's haste toward the time of litany. Similarly, expansion in seeking has three signs: a small amount of listening to music (*samā'*) with great benefit, little service along with great sweetness, and little thought but much vision. (Ansāri, *Sad maydān*)

*　　*　　*

Contraction and expansion are two spiritual states that occur after the servant has passed beyond the states of fear and hope. Contraction, for the knower of God, resembles fear for the beginner, and expansion for the knower is similar to the beginner's hope. The difference between contraction and fear and between expansion and hope is that a man fears something that is to occur in the future, such as the loss of something dear to him or the coming of a sudden affliction. Similarly, he hopes for the coming of something dear to him, for escape from an affliction, or for deliverance from something distasteful in the future. However, both contraction and expansion are spiritual realities that occur at the present moment. The heart of the one who possesses fear or hope is suspended in relation to that which will be, while the present moment of the one who possesses contraction or expansion is drowned in an unseen influx that overcomes him right now.

The attributes of the servants who experience contraction and expansion differ in keeping with the differences among their individual states. There is an influx that results in contraction yet allows other things as well since it is not total; and there are travelers who undergo contraction and have no possibility of perceiving anything but the influx since it has completely removed them from themselves. Thus, one Sufi has said, "I have been filled up." In other words, "Nothing can enter into me." The same is the case with the one who undergoes expansion: He may undergo an expansion that leaves room for creatures, so that he feels no alienation toward most things; or he may undergo an expansion such that nothing has any effect upon him, Abu 'Ali Daqqāq relates that someone once went to visit Abu Bakr Qahtabi. The latter had a son who used to occupy himself with the idle amusements of youth. When the visitor entered, the son and a group of his companions were occupied with their follies. The visitor felt pity for the old man, saying, "Look how this shaykh has been afflicted by this son!" Yet when he went before Abu Bakr, it was as if he was totally unaware of what was going on, and the man marvelled at him. He said, "May I be sacrificed to him who is unaffected by towering and immovable mountains!"

Qahtabi replied, "We were freed from slavery to all things in Eternity-without-beginning."

One minor cause of contraction is an influx that enters the heart and indicates a reprimand or alludes to the servant's deserving chastisement. As a necessary consequence, the heart undergoes contraction. Similarly, it sometimes happens that certain influxes indicate proximity or the arrival of gentleness and gracious welcoming, and as a consequence the heart experiences expansion. On the whole, a person's contraction is one of the same measure as his expansion, and *vice versa.*

The reason for any given contraction is sometimes obscure to its possessor. He may find contraction in his heart, but he does not know its cause or origin. The way of such a person should be submission until this spiritual moment passes, for if he should attempt to negate it or to make it leave before its time is finished, the contraction will only increase. Moreover, such attempts may also be considered a lack of *adab* on his part. When he submits himself to the effect of the spiritual moment, however, the contraction will soon leave him, for as God says, "God contracts and expands, and unto Him you shall be returned" (*Koran,* II:245).

Sometimes, an expansion may arrive suddenly, overtaking its possessor unexpectedly, while he knows of no reason for it. Joy appears in his heart and agitates him. In such a case, his way should be to remain at rest and to observe *adab,* for in such a spiritual moment he faces great danger and must be wary of hidden deception. In reference to this, one of the Sufis has said, "A door was opened for me into expansion, but I suffered a lapse and became veiled from my station." This is why it is also said, "Remain standing on the carpet (*besāt*) and beware of cheerful expansion (*enbesāt*)."

Those who have realized the Truth consider contraction and expansion among those things from which one must seek refuge in God, for in relation to what lies beyond them (i.e., the utter absorption of the servant and his ascension to the Truth) they represent poverty and loss. Jonayd says, "Fear of God contracts me and hope in Him expands me. His Reality gathers me but His Truth disperses me. When He contracts me through fear, He annihilates me from myself; and when He expands me through hope, He gives me back to myself. When He gathers me through Reality, He makes me present with Himself; and when He disperses me through Truth He makes me contemplate 'others', so He conceals me from Himself. In all of this He brings me into motion and leaves me no rest. He fills me with alienation and leaves me no intimacy. Through being present, I taste the flavor of my own experience. Would that He would annihilate me from myself and grant me joy! Would that He would make me absent from myself and grant me ease!" (*Resāla-ye qoshayriyah*)

* * *

The station of contraction is one of the stations of *tawhid.* It possesses three degrees: a degree pertaining to the heart, a degree pertaining to the intellect, and a degree pertaining to the spirit.

The heart contracts first because of the transgressions of the ego, second because of the occurrence of blameworthy thoughts, and third because of the domination of the encroachments of fear. The intellect contracts because of the shocks of the lights of the Attributes. The spirit contracts because of one's melting away before the assaults of the manifestation of the lights of the Essence's Tremendousness. When God contracts the spirit away from itself, it cannot bear to face the vision of Eternity. Thus, it is annihilated, and God does not return it to the possibility of gazing upon temporal things. God says, "And God contracts" (*Koran,* II: 245).

According to Vāseti, "He contracts them away from

Himself through His Might and the fact that the Essence can never be gazed upon face to face by temporal things." The knower of God says, "Contraction is the negation of attributes through His Attributes and the refusal of the Essence by its very nature to be gazed upon by imperfect things." (Ruzbehān, *Mashrab al-arvāh*)

* * *

When the lights of the contemplation of Beauty are diffused within the spirit, when the refreshment of intimacy affects the heart, when the spirit's way is smoothed so that it may travel within the lights of proximity, and when the paths of the Essence and Attributes are no longer blocked for it, then the spirit is in the station of expansion, for it is refreshed by the breeze of the narcissus of union and flies with the wings of hope in the heaven of Beauty. It is not consumed by the splendor of God's Majesty, for God spreads out the carpet of nearness for it and lets it travel upon the mounts of joy within the fields of the eternal realities. As God says, "God contracts and expands, and unto Him shall you be returned" (*Koran*, II:245). One of the Sufis says, "Within contraction and expansion the People of Purity are alienated from the vision of generosities and expanded within the contemplation of the All-Generous." The knower says, "Expansion is for God to send the heart of him who has been contracted by His Tremendousness to the wide-open expanses of the world until it attains to refreshment and intimacy." (*Ibid.*)

* * *

One of the characteristics of the one who contemplates God is the amplification within his breast of the light of intimacy from the World of Holiness. His inmost consciousness expands because God expands it, so that his heart may become dilated by joy and happiness through contemplation. As a result, he is exhilarated by ecstasy, and Beauty is unveiled for him in waves. God says, "God contracts and expands" (*Koran,* II:245). Ebn 'Ātā' says, "He contracts you away from yourself and expands you toward Himself." The knower says, "The contemplator views God in the Attribute of Beauty and is expanded by the refreshment of union and joy through Majesty." However, this expansion is the expansion of contemplation, not the expansion of *tawhid.* The latter expansion is beyond the former, although the former pertains to the shore of the ocean of *tawhid*'s expansion. (*Ibid.*)

*   *   *

When the traveler fills with love and fervent desire, when his inmost consciousness is kindled by the Men of Love who are kindled by expansion, when the state of expansion is kindled by intimacy, when the traveler tastes the' flavor of intimacy and enters into intimacy with God as God shows kindness to Him and manifests Himself to him in the attributes of Beauty and Eternal Comeliness, then he comes to contemplate His Beauty and sees himself as a child in the station of intimacy. He becomes expanded toward God like a child toward its mother. Will you not look at Moses' situation and at what God related concerning him and his words, "Show me (Thyself)" (*Koran,* VII:143), and his words, "It is only Thy trial" (*Koran,* VII: 155)? Abu Sa'id Qorashi says, "The Man of Proximity is permitted to undergo expansion. When intimacy toward other than God and fear of other than Him disappear, and when his soul becomes free and his heart secure, then the traveler is permitted to expand. He expands through what is with God, not through what is with himself, for how is it possible that he should expand through what is with himself since his own self has been annihilated? Thus, his expansion is through what belongs to God, not what belongs to Him." The knower of God says, "Expansion is the disappearance of shame between the lover and the Beloved." (*Ibid.*)

*   *   *

40

Gathering and Dispersion

*If you want to become gathered,
    reflect:
Every moment you keep on increasing your
    dispersion.*

'Attār, Asrār-nāmah

The Sufis call involvement with the world of "I and you" (the world of everything other than God) "dispersion" *(tafreqah)*. Conversely, they call becoming absorbed in God and forgetting everything other than Him the state of "gathering" *(jam')*. To put this another way, they consider attentiveness toward Oneness "gathering" and inclination toward multiplicity "dispersion."

Gathering and dispersion are two inseparable and complementary spiritual states which should exist in equilibrium. Thus, exaggeration of either is not good. On the one hand, if the Sufi should be turned mostly toward the state of gathering, the outward order of his affairs will become disrupted. When this happens, his inward state will also become disturbed and he will be deflected from the Straight Path. Moreover, if his attention becomes constantly turned toward gathering, he may throw off the shirt of servanthood and show his head at the collar of Lordhood, producing harmful effects for himself and others. On the other hand, if the Sufi should incline predominately toward dispersion, the unity of his attentiveness will

41

be destroyed. Ultimately, he may become totally heedless of the state of gathering and be deprived of God.

In regard to the prophets and the elect, sometimes God keeps them in gathering and sometimes in dispersion—for gathering without knowledge is unbelief, while dispersion without gathering is idolatry. Gathering is Reality Itself, but dispersion is the way of servanthood. He who combines these two traits in himself has entered the Straight Path of the *Tariqat* and the *Shari'at*. (Maybodi, *Tafsir*)

> *If the Sufi drinks wine in measure—*
> *to his health!*
> *But if not, let him*
> *forget this business.*
>
> Hāfez

GATHERING AND "GATHERING OF GATHERING"

The term "gathering of gathering" refers to the servant's vision of creation as residing in God. This vision is a contemplative unveiling, not a rational conception. In the state of gathering, all of the Sufi's attention is turned toward God while at the same time he sees both himself and God. In the state of gathering of gathering, the Sufi is so drowned in God that he does not see himself. Whatever he does is done by God, and whatever he says is said by God. As an example of gathering of gathering, the Sufis cite the case of the Holy Prophet, concerning whom God said, "You did not throw when you threw, but God threw" (*Koran*, VIII:17). In this connection Shabestari writes:

> *The Prophet's heart-expanding station*
> *is gathering of gathering.*
> *His spirit-increasing beauty*
> *is the lamp of our gathering.* (Golshan-e rāz)

42

Some Sufis have said that the "science of certainty" is the state of dispersion, the "eye of certainty" the state of gathering, and the "truth of certainty" the state of gathering of gathering (*Rasā'el*, Shāh Ne'matollāh). It can also be said that the vision of God's Acts is dispersion, the vision of His Attributes gathering, and the vision of His Essence gathering of gathering. In another sense, looking at one's own effort is dispersion, attention toward God's effort is gathering, and actualizing annihilation (*fanā'*) is the gathering of gathering.

WORDS OF THE MASTERS CONCERNING GATHERING AND DISPERSION

'Attār's soul is just as dispersed
as Thy tresses—
So gather my scattered soul
with Thine own Face.

'Attār

*　　*　　*

Return from scattered thoughts
and become gathered!
When Ahriman goes,
the angel will come!

Hāfez

The shaykhs and masters of the *Tariqat* have given various definitions of gathering and dispersion, a few of which are quoted below:

Gathering is that which is in God, while disperson is that which belongs to Him. (Bondār ebn Hosayn, *Tabaqāt as-sufiyah*)

Gathering is the very Truth in which all things reside, while dispersion is for the Tsuth to be clear and eparate from falsehood. (Abu Ya'qub Nahrajuri, *Ibid.*)

43

Whoever claims gathering as a trial from God needs to assume the obligation of servanthood's defects. (Bāyazid. *Ibid.*)

Gathering is the mystery of the All-comprehensive, while dispersion is His knowledge. (Bābā Tāher) The commentator writes on this saying:

> "All-comprehensive" is one of God's Names. The "mystery of the All-comprehensive" is the meaning of His words. "I was a Hidden Treasure, so I wanted to be known. Therefore I created the creatures so that I might be known." God spoke these words at the station where "God is and nothing is with Him." In respect of this gathering, dispersion refers to the One Essence coming forth from the Oneness of gathering to the multiplicity of the dispersion of the Names and Attributes. Hence, this dispersion that existed in the uncreated world as knowledge comes to exist in the world of creation as outward entities. (*Sharh-e kalemāt-e qesār*)

He who becomes gathered in God's Desire and does not disperse it with his own attributes has achieved gathering conditioned (by the abandonment of his own desire), but the attributes and description of him who is gathered by God according to His Desire are solely what God desires (i.e. unconditioned by the servant's own desire). (Bābā Tāher, *Ibid.*)

Gathering is the servant's conformity with God's Desire, while dispersion is the servant's conformity with His knowledge. (*Ibid.*)

Gathering is God's knowledge of the objects of His knowledge (i.e., the creatures) before their outward existence, while dispersion is that which the objects of knowledge seek from the realities of gathering (so that they may enter into existence). (*Ibid.*)

Gathering is that thing to whose knowledge the *Koran* and the *Sunnah* give witness, while dispersion is explained by God in His Proof (i.e., in the *Koran*). (*Ibid.*)

Gathering is the Holy Book, while dispersion is the *Sunnah*. That which is gathered and summarized by the Book is explained in detail by the *Sunnah*. (*Ibid.*)

"Dispersion" means scatteredness. It is an allusion to the creatures without reference to God. Some have said that it means the vision of servanthood. (Ebn 'Arabi, *Estelāh as-sufiyah*)

Dispersion means that you scatter your heart through attachment to numerous things, while gathering means that you leave aside all things for the contemplation of the One. One group imagines that gathering lies in gathering provisions and means, but they have remained in everlasting dispersion. Another group knows for certain that gathering provisions and means results in dispersion. They have washed their hands of all things. (Jāmi, *Lavā'eh*)

To be gathered in God is to be dispersed from other than Him, and to be dispersed from other than Him is to be gathered in Him. (Jonayd, *Kashf al-mahjub;* attributed to Nuri in *Tabaqāt as-sufiyah*.)

Gathering is the gathering of dispersed things, while dispersion is the dispersion of gathered things. Thus, when I become gathered, I say, "God and none other." But when I become dispersed, I gaze upon created existence. (Abhari, *Tabaqāt as-sufiyah*)

Gathering and dispersion are two principles, neither of which can do without the other. Thus, he who maintains dispersion without gathering has rejected the Creator, while he who maintains gathering without dispersion has denied the power of the Almighty. But he who combines the two professes *tawhid*. (Abu Nasr Sarrāj, *Ketāb al-loma'*)

Hojviri discusses gathering and dispersion in the following way:

God gathered all mankind together with His sum-

45

mons (i.e., His words, "God summons to the Abode of Peace"/*Koran,* X:26). Then He dispersed them with His words, "And He guides whomsoever He will to a straight path" (*Ibid.*). He called everyone by His summons, but He drove a group away by His Will. He gathered by commanding everyone, then He dispersed by banishing one group to disappointment and accepting another group for good fortune. He also gathered by giving prohibitions, but He dispersed by providing one group with virtue and another with inclination toward affliction. Hence, in this sense, gathering is the reality and mystery of the object of God's Will and Knowledge, while dispersion is the manifestation of His Command. For example, He commanded Abraham to cut Ishmael's throat, but He did not want him to do so. He told Iblis to prostrate himself to Adam, but He did not want him to do so, so he did not. There are many similar cases. Gathering is what He gathers together through His Attributes, while dispersion is what He disperses through His Acts. All of this shows that man's will is ineffectual and that he cannot exercise free choice in the face of God's Will.

In what we have mentioned so far concerning gathering and dispersion, all the Sunnis except the Mu'tazilites are in agreement with the masters of Sufism. After this, there is a difference of opinion in the usage of the terms. One group applies them to *tawhid,* another to the Attributes, and still another to the Acts.

Those who apply these two terms to *tawhid* say that gathering has two degrees, one at the level of God's Attributes and another at the level of the servant's attributes. That which is at the level of God's Attributes is the mystery of *tawhid* and cannot be achieved by the servant through effort, while that which is at the level of the servant's attributes consists of his *tawhid* in accordance with sincerity of intention and sound aspiration. This is the position of Abu 'Ali Rudbāri.

A second group—which applies these terms to the Attributes—says that gathering is God's Attributes and dispersion is His Acts, the servant having no means to acquire either of them since he has no access to Divinity. Gathering is considered to be both God's Essence and Attributes since "gathering means equality at the root of things," and only His Essence and Attributes are equal to Eternity—for they can only be considered as separate when they are discussed and set one above the other by the creatures. In other words, He possesses eternal Attributes specific to Himself, Attributes which reside in Him and whose existence pertains to Him. He and His Attributes are not two, since no distinction or multiplicity is permitted in His Oneness. Hence, gathering is permitted only in this sense. As for dispersion in properties, that pertains to the Acts of God which are all diverse in their properties. The property of one is existence, while that of another is nonexistence, for only in the case of things at the level of possible existence is the property of one annihilation and that of another subsistence.

Still another group applies these terms to science (*'elm*). They say that gathering is the science of *tawhid*, while dispersion is the science of the statutes of the *Shari'at*. In this sense, the science of the principles of Islam is gathering, while that of their ramifications is dispersion. Something like this was expressed by one of the masters as follows: "Gathering is that concerning which the men of knowledge agree, while dispersion is that concerning which they disagree."

Again, in the course of their expressions and allusions most of the authorities in Sufism employ "dispersion" to mean those things which can be acquired and "gathering" to mean graces of God, the two terms meaning effort on the one hand and contemplation on the other. That which the servant attains through effort is all dispersion, but that which is the pure grace and guidance of God is gathering.

47

The servant's greatness lies in this: the existence of his acts and the possibility of his effort can be delivered from the bane of self-activity through God's Beauty, so that he finds his acts drowned in God's blessings and his effort negated by His guidance. Then he resides in God and God transforms his attributes, while his acts become attributed solely to God. In this way, he is delivered from his own activity and acquisition.

This station is referred to in the words of God which have been narrated by the Prophet, "My servant never ceases to come nigh to Me through supererogatory works until I love him. Then when I love him, I become his ears, his eyes, his hands, his support and his tongue. He hears through Me, sees through Me, speaks through Me and grasps through Me." God says: When Our servant comes nigh to Us through effort, We bring him into Our Love, annihilate him from his existence, and cleanse him of his relationship with his acts. Then he hears what he hears through Us, says what he says through Us, sees what he sees through Us and grasps what he grasps through Us. In other words, in his remembrance (*dhekr*) of Us he is overcome by Our remembrance of him. His acquisition of his remembrance is annihilated and Our remembrance takes control. The human side of his remembrance is eliminated, so his remembrance becomes Our remembrance, and in his spiritual states that attribute predominates which was voiced by Bāyazid, "Glory be to Me! Glory be to Me! How tremendous is My station!" His words were his own words, but the speaker was God. . . .

Hence, it is permissible for a love to come from God and dominate the servant's heart such that, because of its overpowering force and intensity, the intellect and natural disposition are incapable of tolerating it. At this point, the servant's affairs leave the domain of his own acquisition. This spiritual degree is referred to as "gathering." Thus, when the Prophet was immersed and overcome, an act was accomplished at his hands. God avoided attributing that act to him and said, "That was My act not yours, even if it appeared to be your act ("You did not throw when you threw, but God threw" [*Koran,* VIII:17]). O Mohammad! You did not throw that handful of dust in the enemy's face, I threw it." In a similar way, a certain act was accomplished through David. God said, "David killed Goliath" (*Koran,* II:251), since the act was performed in the state of dispersion. There is a great difference between God's attributing His Act to the servant, who is a locus of ills and temporal events, and His attributing it to Himself, who is eternal and transcends all ills.

Hence, when a person performs an act that is not of the same kind as other human acts, undoubtedly the agent of that act is God. The miracles of the prophets and the saints all occur in such a manner. Therefore, "ordinary" acts are all dispersion, but "extraordinary" acts are all gathering. Thus, it is not an "ordinary" act for a man to be taken to the station of "Two Bows' Length" (*Koran,* LIII:9) in a single night: That is nothing but God's Act. Not being burnt by fire is extraordinary, so that also is nothing but God's Act. In this way, God has given these miracles to His prophets and saints. He has attributed His own Acts to them, and their acts to Himself—for the Acts of His friends are His Acts. Swearing the oath of allegiance to His friends is to swear it to Him, and obeying them is to obey Him. Thus, God said, "Those who swear allegiance to thee swear allegiance in truth to God" (*Koran,* XLVIII:10), and "Whosoever obeys the Messenger, thereby obeys God" (*Koran,* IV: 80). God's saints are gathered within their inmost consciousness, but dispersed in the manifestation of their conduct. Thus, their love is firm through the gathering of their inmost consciousnesses, while their performance of the duties of servanthood is put in order through the dispersion of outward manifestation. In this connection, one of the great

49

masters has spoken as follows concerning the state of gathering:

> *Thou hast been realized within my inmost con-*
> *sciousness,*
> *while my tongue whispers to Thee.*
> *So we are gathered in some respects*
> *but dispersed in others.*
> *Although reverence has kept Thee hidden*
> *from the glance of my eyes,*
> *Ecstasy has made Thee near*
> *to my heart.*

The poet calls the coming together of inmost conscious-nesses "gathering" and the prayers of the tongue "disper-sion." Then, he subtly points to both gathering and dispersion within himself and makes himself their basis.

There remains to be explained the difference that ex-ists between ourselves and that group which says that the manifestation of gathering negates dispersion, since the two are opposites. The reason given for this is that when the overpowering force of God's guidance takes com-mand, the domain of acquisition and effort is overthrown. But this view wrongly nullifies man's actions, since as long as the servant retains the ability to act and the power to acquire, and as long as he continues to strive, these things will not be negated. That is, gathering is not separate from dispersion. The two of them are like light and the sun, or accident and substance, or the attribute and the thing that possesses it. In other words, effort is not separate from guidance, nor the *Shari'at* from the Truth (*haqiqat*), nor finding from seeking. However, sometimes effort may pre-cede guidance and other times it may follow it. When a person's effort comes first, his hardship is great, since he is absent from God. But when a person's effort comes after-wards, he undergoes no suffering or difficulty since he is in God's Presence.

Those who negate the very substance of activity by negating the doctrine of the effectiveness of works have made a terrible error. It is quite permissible that the servant reach a degree where he gazes upon all of his own praiseworthy acts as defective and imperfect. But even if he sees his own praiseworthy attributes as defective and deficient, he still must see his own blameworthy attributes as even more defective.

I mention these things because a group of the ignorant have fallen into an error which is near to alienation from the religion. They say that nothing of spiritual realization can be attained by our own effort; that our acts and obedience are deficient and our striving imperfect; and that it is better not to act than to act. We answer them as follows: You agree with us that each thing we do is an act and that acts are defective and a source of baneful results. But not doing something must itself be considered an act. Since both doing and not-doing are acts, and since acts are defective, how can not-doing be considered better than doing? This is a manifest loss and a terrible deception.

Hence, there exists a clear distinction between unbelief and faith: Both believer and unbeliever agree that their acts are defective. The believer, in order to obey God's command, considers doing better than not-doing. However, the unbeliever, because of his disobedience of God's command, considers not-doing better than doing.

In this sense, "gathering" means that, while a person sees the baneful effects of dispersion, he does not let go of the properties of dispersion. In contrast, "dispersion" means that, while veiled from gathering, he is able to turn dispersion into gathering.

In this connection, Mozayyen the Elder says, "Gathering is election, while dispersion is servanthood. The two are connected to each other, never separated." God's election of the servant is the servant's gathering, while his servanthood is his dispersion. These two are never separate, since the sign of election is the observance of servant-hood. If he who calls people to perform works is not himself engaged in works, then his call is false. It is permissible for the servant to be freed from the difficulty of striving and the pain of effort which he experiences while carrying out what is necessary in the way of his spiritual discipline and his obligations to God, but it is not permissible for the spiritual discipline and the performing of one's duty themselves to be eliminated in the state of gathering, unless through a clear excuse applying to all the statutes of the *Shari'at*.

It may be more clear to say that gathering is of two kinds. One is called "sound gathering," and the other "broken gathering." Sound gathering is the protection of the servant by God when the servant is in the midst of the overpowering force of a spiritual state and of the strength of ecstasy and tumult of ardor. He commands him to perform outward acts and maintains his observance of them; that is, He adorns him with the performance of the spiritual discipline. Thus, Sahl ebn 'Abdollāh, Abu Hafs Haddād, Abol-'Abbās Sayyāri (the founder of the school), Bāyazid Bastāmi, Abu Bakr Shebli, Abol-Hasan Hosri and many others were constantly overcome. But when the time for the ritual prayer arrived, they would return to a normal state of consciousness. Then, after performing the prayer, they would once again be overcome. In the locus of dispersion, you are you, so you obey His commands. And when He attracts you, it is even more appropriate that He make certain you perform His commands: first, so that the signs of your servanthood may remain, and second, so that He should act according to His promise never to abrogate Mohammad's *Shari'at*.

In contrast to "sound gathering," "broken gathering" occurs when the servant, while being overcome by God, becomes utterly confused and distraught, like a madman. As a result, one of these two servants is worthy of praise, while the other has an excuse. The days of him who is worthy of praise are tremendously full of light and much stronger than those of him who has an excuse.

In short, you should know that gathering is not a special station (*maqām*) or a single state (*ḥāl*), for gathering occurs when aspiration becomes gathered by the reality of the Object of one's quest. It is unveiled to certain travelers in the midst of the "stations" and to others during the "states." In either case, when he who undergoes gathering desires his gathering to remain, he attains this goal by negating his desires, for dispersion is separation from God, but gathering is union with Him.

Gathering and dispersion take place in relation to all things. For example, the gathering of the aspiration of Jacob toward Joseph was such that other than aspiration for him, no other aspiration remained. The gathering of the aspiration of Majnun toward Laylā was such that when he did not see her, the whole world and all existent things appeared to him in her form. There are similar examples. For instance, one day Bāyazid was in his cell. Someone came and said, "Is Bāyazid in the house?" He answered, "Is there anyone in the house but God?" One of the masters relates that a darvish came to Mecca and sat contemplating the *Ka'aba* for a whole year. He neither ate, drank, slept nor went to make his purifications. Since his aspiration had been gathered toward the vision of God's house, his body's need for food and his vital spirit's need for drink were totally eliminated.

The root of all this is that God has divided and separated the substance of His Love, which was one. He allotted one of the particles of that whole to each of His friends in proportion to the extent of his captivation by Him. He has covered that particle of Love with the armor of human nature, the clothing of animal nature, the wrap of the temperament, and the veil of the spirit. Then, through its power, that particle transforms the things that have become attached to it into its own attribute, so that the whole lover becomes totally Beloved, and all his movements and

53

moments gain His qualities. That is why the Lords of the Meanings and the Possessors of the Tongue have named that state "gathering." In this connection Hallāj says:

> Here am I! Here am I,
> my Lord, my Master!
> Here am I! Here am I,
> my Goal, my Reality!
> O very substance of my existence!
> O ultimate goal of my aspiration!
> O my speech and my unspoken allusions!
> O my every communication!
> O all of my all!
> O my hearing, my speech!
> O my whole!
> O my parts and particles!

For the one who sees his own attributes as a loan, affirming his own existence is a disgrace. To turn one's regard toward the two worlds is for him a sign of shame. In the eyes of his aspiration, all existence is insignificant.

For the sake of providing more precise terminology and a more powerful expression, certain Possessors of the Tongue use the term "gathering of gathering." In terms of expression, this is a beautiful phrase. But in terms of its meaning, it is better not to ascribe gathering to gathering— for gathering would have to be dispersed to become gathered again. When gathering becomes gathered, this shows that there was dispersion. But gathering does not in fact depart from its own state. Moreover, this expression may invite accusations, since he who is gathered does not look above and below and outside of himself. Do you not see that the two worlds were shown to the Prophet during his Night Journey, but that he did not pay them any regard? For he was gathered in the state of gathering, and the person in this state witnesses no dispersion. That is why

God said, "His eye swerved not nor swept away" (*Koran,* LIII:17). (*Kashf al-mahjub*)

* * *

The first station of the Sufis in gathering is that the servant's aspiration becomes gathered. In other words, he makes all of his aspirations into a single aspiration. The common people seek all kinds of things with their aspirations, and as a result their aspirations become dispersed. But the Sufis occupy their aspiration with a single thing. As a result, their aspiration is gathered and not scattered. This is because as much as the servant is outwardly occupied with something—whether that thing is this world, the next world, or God—he is unconcerned with other things. As long as he does not free his aspiration from the next world, he cannot occupy himself with this world; and as long as he does not free it from this world, he cannot occupy himself with the next. Likewise, as long as he does not free it from both of these, he cannot occupy himself with God. . . .

When the servant collects himself away from all these aspirations and attains a certain gathering so that all of his aspirations are in conformity with God, then his outward being becomes subordinated to his inward being. When his inward being becomes subject to God, his outward being becomes subject to His service, so that nothing but occupation with God remains in his outward and inward being. God then takes care of his other occupations. The world is no longer his companion, creatures are no longer in harmony with him, Satan no longer has any hold upon him, and his own ego ceases to dispute with him. This is the state of effort and spiritual discipline.

That gathering which the Sufis claim as their own occurs when the servant's gathering becomes his spiritual state. In other words, his aspirations are no longer scattered. God—or conformity with and obedience to God's affairs—takes over his consciousness to such an extent that he does not become dispersed by any occupation; nor is it necessary for him to make a personal effort to collect his aspirations together. On the contrary, they remain collected by themselves. Thus, he has no need to undertake the effort of gathering. When his aspiration becomes gathered, it becomes so because he contemplates its Gatherer. Since the Gatherer is One, the gathering also possesses but a single property. This gathering becomes established only through God, not through any others.

The dispersion that follows this gathering takes place when the servant becomes separated from his aspirations toward worldly pleasure and from his seeking ease and joy. Hence, a dispersion takes place between him and his ego, so that it no longer controls his activities.

Certain of the Sufis have said that as long as the creatures are with themselves, they are dispersed; but when they become absent from themselves, they are gathered.

Others say that gathering is the state of nonexistence that the creatures once had when there was nothing but God's Knowledge that they would come into existence. And dispersion is the state that brought them from nonexistence to existence. (*Kholāsa-ye sharh-e ta'arrof*)

* * *

In Sufi terminology, the word "gathering" signifies the removal of separation, the nullification of all attributions and the contemplation of God alone. The term "dispersion" alludes to the existence of separation, the affirmation of both servanthood and Lordship, and the distinction between God and creation. Thus, gathering without dispersion is pure heresy, while dispersion without gathering is utter idolatry. But gathering along with dispersion is the manifest truth and sound belief in that the properties of gathering belong to the spirit, while those of dispersion belong to the body. As long as the body and the spirit remain related through their composition, the combination of gathering and dispersion is necessitated by existence. Hence, the realized knower of God (*'āref*) is constantly in a state of gathering within his spirit, which is the locus of contemplation, and in a station of dispersion within his body, which is the instrument of spiritual discipline. . . .

Vāseti says, "When you look at yourself, you are in dispersion; when you look at your Lord, you are in gathering; but when you reside in the Other, you are annihilated from yourself without gathering or dispersion." The Sufis call this last state "gathering of gathering." Whoever looks at his own effort in obedience is in the station of dispersion, while whoever looks at God's bounty is in the station of gathering. But whoever becomes totally annihilated from himself and his own acts is in the station of gathering of gathering.

Abu 'Ali Daqqāq says, "Whatever is ascribed to you is dispersion, but whatever is negated from you is gathering." Jonayd says, "Proximity through ecstacy is gathering, while absence within human nature is dispersion." The gist of all these allusions is that when the creatures become hidden and concealed by the overpowering force of God's Self-manifestation and the overwhelming mastery of the contemplation of God, gathering has occurred. However, when God becomes hidden and concealed by the vision of the existence of the creatures, then dispersion exists.

Abu Sa'id Kharrāz says, "The meaning of 'gathering' is that God makes Himself existent within their own selves, just as they are existent within themselves for themselves. Or rather, He naughts their existence for themselves so that their existence belongs to Him. This is the meaning of His words, 'I am his ears and eyes and hand; so through Me he hears, through Me he sees, and through Me he grasps.' Before this, they used to act in themselves for themselves, but now they act in God for God." ('Ezzod-Din Kāshāni, *Mesbāh al-hedāyah*)

*   *   *

Whatever the servant acquires (i.e., through performing the duties of servanthood) and all that is appropriate to the states of human nature pertain to dispersion. Whatever comes from God (i.e., the manifestation of unseen realities and the bestowing of kindness and graciousness) pertains to gathering. But such things are the lowest states of the Sufis in gathering and dispersion, for they all occur at the level of the contemplation of God's Acts. When God makes a servant the witness of his own acts of obedience and disobedience, he is qualified by dispersion. But when He makes him the witness of His own Acts, then he is in the station of gathering. To affirm creation is a property of dispersion, but to affirm God is an attribute of gathering.

The servant cannot escape either dispersion or gathering since he who has no dispersion cannot perform his acts of worship, while he who has no gathering has no knowledge. God's words, "Thee alone we worship" (*Koran,* I:5) allude to dispersion, while "Thee alone we pray for succor" (*ibid.*) alludes to gathering. When the servant addresses God with the tongue of intimate discourse— whether in request, supplication, praise, thanksgiving, or asking forgiveness—he is in the state of dispersion. But when he speaks to Him in his inmost consciousness and listens to Him in his heart, he receives what he receives from Him in the station of gathering.

As for "gathering of gathering," that is higher than gathering, although there are differences among the Sufis in keeping with the distinctions among their states and the diversity of their spiritual degrees. When someone affirms both his own self and creation but sees them residing in God, that is gathering. But when he is snatched away from the vision of both creation and himself so that he is totally unaware of all things because of what becomes manifested to him and overcomes him from the Sultan of Reality, that is the gathering of gathering.

Dispersion is to see "others" as belonging to God; gathering is to see others in God; and gathering of gathering is to be totally obliterated from all things and not to have awareness of other than God at the time of the overwhelming manifestation of Reality.

Beyond this, there is a subtle spiritual station that the Sufis refer to as the "second dispersion." It occurs when the servant is given back sobriety at the time of the performance of his religious duties so that he may accomplish these duties at the proper time. Thus, his performance of his duties is ascribed to God in God, not to the servant in himself. In all of this, he sees himself in God's total control. He sees Him as the Originator of his essence and knows that He bestows his states and acts through His Knowledge and Will.

Some Sufis have also employed the terms dispersion and gathering to refer to God's turning about of the creatures from state to state. That is, He gathered all of them together in His controlling power and transforming force since He created their essences and bestowed their attributes. Then, He dispersed them within different degrees. He gives one group felicity and drives another group far away. He attracts one group to Himself, bestows upon another group proximity to Himself and places another group at a far distance. But the kinds of His Acts are infinite and cannot be described. *(Resāla-ye qoshayriyah)*

*　　*　　*

God says, "You did not throw when you threw but God threw" (*Koran,* VIII:17). Gathering is that which nullifies dispersion, cuts off allusions, and towers over water and clay. It is achieved after sound consolidation, freedom from variegation, deliverance from the vision of duality, incompatibleness with the perception of defectiveness,

59

and purification from the vision of seeing through these things.

Gathering has three degrees: that of knowledge (*'elm*), that of existence, and that of Entity. The gathering of knowledge is the naughting of all knowledge attained through evidence within unadulterated knowledge from His Presence. The gathering of existence is the naughting, through total effacement, of the outermost limit of union within Being Itself. Finally, the gathering of Entity is the naughting of everything to which allusions can be made within God's Essence in truth. Gathering is the last of the stations of the travelers and one of the shores of the Ocean of *tawhid*. (Ansāri, *Manāzel as-sā'erin*)

*   *   *

The battlefield of gathering is born from the battle-field of jealousy. God says, "Then leave them alone, playing the games into which they have plunged" (*Koran*, VI:92). Gathering is for three things to be delivered from dispersion: the heart, the intention, and the present moment.

The gathering of the heart has three signs: not wanting increase, estrangement from the creatures, and weariness with life. The gathering of intention has three signs: sweetness deriving from service to God, desire for knowledge, and considering one's undertaking agreeable. And the gathering of the present moment has three signs: sweetness from constant prayer, the birth of wisdom, and correct discernment of human nature. (Ansāri, *Sad maydān*)

*   *   *

The reality of gathering is a sign of unification, and unification is a sign of love. Dispersion is a sign of duality, and duality is alienation. Whatever brightness the candle gives is a result of gathering. The wax gives no light without fire, and fire without wax is useless to illuminate the meeting. This gathering is the Path, and beyond it is the

Truth, which is the naughting of human nature. (Ansāri, *Rasā'el*)

* * *

Maybodi comments on the *Koranic* verse, "You did not throw when you threw, but God threw" as follows: The "throwing" of the servant is dispersion, while God's throwing is gathering. Total dispersion without gathering is the belief of those who believe in absolute free will, while total gathering without dispersion is the belief of those who believe in predestination. Gathering and dispersion together form the way of the believers, and it is the correct way. Those who maintain absolute free will believe that they possess choice and ability, so they step beyond their own limits. The predestinarians are those who have lost their heads because of the controlling force of the archangelic world, so they do not see secondary causes and allow themselves no free choice. (*Tafsir*)

* * *

God says, "Say: 'If you love God, follow me, and God will love you'" (*Koran*, III:31). "If you love God" is dispersion, and "God will love you" is gathering. The first is to serve the *Shari'at*, while the second is the generosity of the *Haqiqat*. Since service goes from the servant up to God while generosity comes from God down to the servant, whatever goes up to God from the servant is dispersion and is connected to scatteredness. But whatever comes down from God is gathering and welcome; it is pure of every bias and free of every defect. (*Ibid.*)

* * *

He who is in dispersion looks at the creatures and does not see the divine causes of affairs. Thus, he is never at rest from his troubles or free from people's enmity. But he who is in gathering looks at God and knows that God is One, that all acts come from one place, and that decrees enter only from this door. Dispersion is for the servant's

61

desire to be different from God's desire, while gathering is for the servant's desire to be one with His desire. (*Ibid.*)

* * *

Gathering is the gathering of one's aspiration toward God, the presence of the heart with God, and the contemplation by the inmost consciousness of God without the interference of the self or any lapse. The reality of gathering is that you contemplate the Essence through the Essence, not that you contemplate the lights of the Attributes in the vision of the Essence. Abu Sa'id al-Qorashi says, "Gathering is the very essence of *tawhid.*" The knower of God says, "When you perceive the Essence through the Essence, that is gathering." (Ruzbehān, *Mashrab al-arvāh*)

* * *

Dispersion is dispersion of aspiration in thoughts and accidents. Its reality is that you return from the vision of the Essence to the vision of the Attributes. God says, "God bears witness that there is no god but He" (*Koran,* III:18). He gives news of His Essence with the words "God," then He gives news of His Attributes with the words, "there is no god but He." One of the Sufis cites the same verse in explaining the reality of gathering and dispersion. But he says that all of the above refers to gathering. Then the next words, "and the angels and men possessed of knowledge," refer to dispersion. It has also been said that gathering lies in knowledge of God (*ma're-fat*), while dispersion lies within the spiritual states and stations. The knower says, "Dispersion is for you to be in servanthood, while gathering is for you to be in Lordship." (*Ibid.*)

* * *

The "eye of gathering" is that you see the light of the Attributes in the guise of the Acts, just as Moses saw the

62

light of God's theophany in the mountain: "And when his Lord displayed His theophany to the mountain" (*Koran*, VII:143). God also spoke to him from the tree: "Moses, I am God, the Lord of all the world's inhabitants" (*Koran*, XXVIII:30). The Prophet said, "I saw my Lord in the fairest form." One of the Sufis said, "I have never looked at anything without seeing God within it." The knower says, "The eye of gathering is the reality of unification. Have you not pondered how He spoke to His Prophet: 'You did not throw when you threw, but God threw?'" (*Ibid.*)

* * *

In the station of "gathering of gathering," the knower in his contemplation sees God in His Essence and Attributes; he sees both the Essence and the Attributes in the property of annihilation, and he sees the Attributes in the Essence and the Essence in the Attributes. This takes place when the Essence becomes unveiled and the Attributes depart from him (i.e., the knower) through Power, Overwhelming Force, Severity, and Domination. The knower says, "This station is one of the realities of the theophany of Lordship; it produces in the knower the love for the contemplation of Eternity forever." (*Ibid.*)

TWO ANECDOTES ON GATHERING AND DISPERSION

One of the Sufis sent a prayer-carpet to Bāyazid and asked him to pray on it. Bāyazid wrote back to him, "I gathered together the worship of the ancients and the later folk and placed them upon my pillow. Then I was asked to lay my head upon the pillow so that my sleep might sanction all that worship." The point of the story can be seen in the fact that the Sufi wrote from the viewpoint of dispersion, while Bāyazid answered from that of gathering. (Maybodi, *Tafsir*)

63

It has been related in various sources that one day Jonayd and Shebli were walking along a road. Jonayd said to Shebli, "Be with God for a time until I come back." Shebli occupied himself with reciting the *Koran*. Jonayd returned and shouted, "I told you to occupy yourself with God!" Shebli replied, "I thought that by reading the *Koran* I would be occupied with Him." Jonayd said, "Do you not know that whoever is with God cannot speak?" Shebli spoke from dispersion and Jonayd replied from the standpoint of gathering. (*Ibid.*)

Intoxication and Sobriety

The subject of the spiritual states of "intoxication" (*sokr, masti*) and "sobriety" (*sahv, hoshyāri*) is an important and complicated one in Sufism. Sufi masters have held different opinions concerning these states in keeping with their own spiritual attainments. Some of them have held that intoxication is superior, while others have spoken of the preeminence of sobriety. This chapter will attempt to clarify the meaning of these two terms and to present the views of various masters concerning them. The hope is that these words will be agreeable to the travelers on the path toward God and aid them on the way.

INTOXICATION

> *When you have become headless and footless*
> *in the way of the Almighty,*
> *You will be transformed into His light*
> *from head to foot.*
>
> Hāfez

The word *sokr* means "intoxication" or "drunkenness." In Sufi terminology, it refers to a spiritual state in which the Sufi loses awareness of everything except the Beloved.

More generally, it can be said that there are two kinds of intoxication: one of which is "artificial" and the other of which is "natural." Artificial intoxication results from the drinking of alcoholic beverages or the consuming of certain natural or man-made poisons. It is referred to here as "artificial" since it poisons the brain and produces an unnatural or artificial feeling of well-being.

In former times (and to a certain extent in our own times), certain people who appeared to be Sufis but who lacked the benefit of natural intoxication were in the habit of employing artificial intoxication in its place. By means of wine and especially hashish, they sought God-given ecstasy.

> *They place upon themselves the shame*
> *of hashish and opium*
> *To escape for an instant*
> *the shackles of existence.*
>
> *Rumi*

This type of intoxication, however, does not last and disappears with the effect of the intoxicant. Through its poisoning of the body and causing of addiction, this kind of intoxication makes people lazy, uncaring and indolent, and sometimes results in psychological disorders. The secondary symptoms of this kind of addiction include fleeing from the realities and facts of life and becoming cut off from the foundations and values of the human state. For this reason, the use of intoxicating substances is forbidden in Islam.

As opposed to "artificial intoxication," "natural intoxication" occurs only through God's assistance and attraction. In artificial intoxication, the light of reason is dimmed by the darkness of the poisons ingested, but in natural intoxication reason's light is obliterated by the overpowering Light of God.

> *Behold this intoxication and leave aside reason.*
> *Behold these celestial sweet-meats and leave aside*
> *traditional authority.*
> *Do not exert yourself so much for mere*
> *bread and vegetables!*
>
> *Rumi*

Natural intoxication results in the "elimination" of discernment, but only in the sense that the traveler's attention is turned solely toward God. The Sufi can no longer distinguish between good and evil or profit and loss. He has no awareness of unbelief or faith, no use for customs and habits. He cannot discern the lawful from the unlawful or perfection from imperfection.

> *In intoxication and selflessness,*
> *you will reach a place*
> *Where acts of worship are overthrown*
> *and allusions completely vanish.*
>
> *'Erāqi*

SOBRIETY

> *Even kings are the slaves*
> *of Thy drunken eyes,*
> *And the sober ruined*
> *by the wine of Thy lips.*
>
> *Hāfez*

The word *sahv* signifies the return to sobriety after intoxication. As a Sufi term, it refers to the sobriety of the

67

traveler after his return from the spiritual state of intoxication. *Sahv* also means the dispersal of clouds or a clear day. In this sense, one could say that sobriety signifies the clearing of the clouds of intoxication from the traveler's mind. Thus, sobriety is a spiritual state beyond and more exalted than intoxication.

One must note carefully that "sobriety" in this technical sense does *not* refer to the state of soberness before intoxication when the Sufi is present with himself but absent from God. In the state of true sobriety, which occurs after intoxication, the Sufi is present both with himself and with God. In other words, he is both with God and with the creation.

In the state of sobriety, the Sufi is in love with beauty. He is the servant of all men; he loves everyone. He is not troubled by the bad things he sees in people and embraces both friend and stranger. He has no anger or wrath, no worries or cares. He is always happy and joyful, and his mind is never upset. He does not see his own self intruding but rather sees all things as God.

Even though the Sufi in the state of sobriety feels close to everyone, he also sees himself as a stranger to all men. He is with everyone, yet he is totally alone. Whether he is in a social situation or alone makes no difference to him; events have no effect upon him. His spiritual state sings this verse:

> *After this, my face will gaze upon the mirror*
> *of Beauty's attributes: that is where*
> *The news of the manifestation of my essence*
> *is to be found.*
>
> *Hāfez*

Some Sufis have called this sobriety the "second dispersion" and the state of soberness before intoxication (and annihilation) the "first dispersion." They have also called this sobriety "natural dispersion" and the "station of gathering of gathering," while calling annihilation the level of "gathering."

THE VIEWS OF THE ADVOCATES OF INTOXICATION

Ask for the mystery behind the veil
from the drunken profligates:
No high-stationed ascetic
possesses such a state.

Hāfez

Bāyazid and his followers (known as the "Tayfuri-yah") were advocates of intoxication, which they preferred to sobriety. In their view, sobriety is based upon the consolidation and equilibrium of human attributes, while these are precisely the greatest veils between man and God. Conversely, in their view, intoxication is based upon the disappearance of that imperfection and affliction known as the "attributes of human nature." Intoxication presupposes the abandonment of choice, of the management of one's own affairs, as well as the annihilation of all self-centered activity. Thus, it is a more perfect state than sobriety.

The advocates of intoxication argue further that when the prophet David was in a state of sobriety and performed a certain act, God attributed that act to him by saying, "David killed Goliath" (*Koran,* II:251). However, when Mohammad was in a state of intoxication and performed an act, God attributed it to Himself, "You did not throw when you threw, but God threw" (*Koran,* VIII:17). Thus, David subsisted through his own self and was anchored in his own attributes, so God said to him as a kind of favor, "You did it." But the Prophet subsisted through God and was naughted from his own attributes, so God said to him, "We did what We did." The attribution of the servant's act to God is better than the attribution of God's act to the servant, for when God's act is attributed to the servant, he subsists through his own self-existence. However, when the servant's act is attributed to God, he subsists through God. (Adapted from *Kashf al-mahjub*)

THE VIEWS OF THE ADVOCATES OF SOBRIETY

Jonayd and his followers were advocates of sobriety, which they considered higher than intoxication. They held that intoxication is based upon the disruption of one's normal state and the loss of human awareness and choice, and that a person who is searching for Reality must be in a state of mental equilibrium.

Jonayd and Hallāj are said to have had the following conversation concerning sobriety and intoxication:

When Hallāj was overcome by his spiritual state, he left his master, 'Amr ebn 'Othmān, and came to Jonayd. Jonayd said to him, "Why did you come?"

Hallāj answered, "In order to be your companion."

Jonayd said, "We do not accept madmen as our companions, for companionship must be genuine. But if you become our companion, you will do to us what you did to Sahl Tostari and 'Amr: you will break the covenant."

Hallāj replied, "O master! Sobriety and intoxication are both attributes of the servant. As long as the servant's attributes have not been annihilated, he continues to be veiled from his Lord."

Jonayd answered, "O son of Mansur! You are mistaken concerning sobriety and intoxication, for everyone agrees that sobriety denotes man's proper state with God. Thus, it cannot be his own attribute

or acquisition. O son of Mansur! I see a good deal of
nonsense and meaningless expression in your words."
(*Kashf al-mahjub*)

Hojviri explains:

> Intoxication brings about baneful results, since it
> disrupts a person's spiritual states. Soundness disap-
> pears and one loses touch with one's own self. All
> spiritual realities depend upon the seeker, who is their
> foundation, since it is he who becomes annihilated or
> attains to subsistence, who becomes obliterated or
> firmly established. Thus, if a person does not have a
> sound state, he cannot experience spiritual realiza-
> tion. (*Kashf al-mahjub*)

Hojviri also writes:

> The hearts of the People of God must be disen-
> gaged from everything that might hold them back.
> But blindness will never allow a person to be freed
> from the shackles of things or to be delivered from
> their baneful effects. The reason people remain at-
> tached to things is that they do not see them as they
> really are. If they did, they would be freed from them.
> Correct vision is of two kinds: in the first kind,
> you behold the thing with an eye toward its subsis-
> tence. In the second kind, you behold it with an eye
> toward its annihilation. If you look with the eye of
> subsistence, you will see that all things are imperfect
> in their subsistence, since in their very state of subsis-
> tence they do not subsist through themselves. If you
> look with the eye of annihilation, you will see that all
> things are annihilated in relation to God's subsis-
> tence. Both of these attributes will thus turn you away
> from existent things. It is to this that the Prophet re-
> ferred in his prayer, "O God, show us all things as
> they truly are!" Whoever sees things as they truly are

will find peace. This is also the meaning of God's words, "Take heed, O you who have eyes!" (*Koran,* LIX:2).

Such vision cannot be acquired except in a state of sobriety. The People of Intoxication know nothing of these things. Hence, when Moses was in a state of intoxication, he was not able to bear a single one of God's theophanies but fell down in a swoon (*Koran,* VII:143). However, the Prophet was in a state of sobriety, and during his Night Journey (*me'rāj*) he experienced God's theophanies constantly from Mecca to the station of "Two Bow's Length" (*Koran,* LIII:9). Yet at each moment he became more conscious and more awake. (*Kashf al-mahjub*)

Hojviri has also written:

Intoxication cannot be acquired by human effort, and it is useless to ask someone to strive after that which he cannot attain and absurd for someone to try to imitate it. (*Kashf al-mahjub*)

Again Hojviri writes:

Intoxication and becoming overwhelmed by God are not within the domain of acquisition; that is, one cannot attain them through spiritual combat and effort. Effort alone cannot be the cause of intoxication. However, one can perform spiritual combat to attain sobriety. For this reason, the Possessor of Sobriety cannot accept the validity of intoxication; that would be absurd. . . . (*Kashf al-mahjub*)

The lengthy discussion below, taken again from Hojviri's *Kashf al-mahjub,* elucidates a number of vital points about the relationship between intoxication and sobriety:

My master, who followed Jonayd, used to say that intoxication is the playground of children, while sobriety is the annihilation-ground of men. As for me, who am 'Ali ebn 'Othmān al-Jollābi, I agree with my master. The perfection of the state of the "possessor of intoxication" is sobriety, and the lowest rank in sobriety is to see the imperfection of human nature. Thus, a sobriety that shows us a baneful state is better than an intoxication which is itself that state.

They say that in the beginning of his spiritual life Abu 'Othmān Maghrebi lived alone for twenty years in the desert in a manner that men cannot imagine. Hardship wasted his physical frame. Each of his eyes became as small as the eye of a needle, and he no longer even resembled a human being. After twenty years, he was commanded to search out the companionship of men. He said to himself, "It will be more blessed if I begin this companionship with the People of God and those who dwell in the vicinity of His house," so he set out for Mecca. The masters there became aware in their hearts of his coming and came out of the city to welcome him. They found him outwardly transformed, in a state where he hardly resembled a human creature. They said, "O Abu 'Othmān, for twenty years you have lived in such a manner that Adam and his progeny are dumb-founded by your situation. Tell us why you went, what you saw, what you found, and why you returned!"

He replied, "I went because of intoxication; I saw its baneful effects; I found despair, and I returned out of helplessness."

All of the masters said to him, "O Abu 'Othmān! After you, it is forbidden for people to discuss intoxication and sobriety, for you have done the subject full justice and shown intoxication's baneful effects."

Intoxication is to imagine that you have undergone annihilation, while in reality your own attributes remain. Thus, it is a veil. Sobriety, however, is the vision of your subsistence at the same time that your attributes have been annihilated. Thus, it is true unveiling.

In short, it is absurd for someone to think that intoxication is nearer to annihilation than sobriety, for intoxication is an attribute over and above sobriety. As long as the servant's attributes increase, he has no news of annihilation. But when they begin to decrease, then there is some hope for him. This then is the final word about intoxication and sobriety on this path.

The following story is related about Bāyazid. Yahyā ebn Ma'ādh wrote him a letter asking, "What do you say about someone who becomes intoxicated from a single drop of the Ocean of Love?" Bāyazid wrote back, "What do *you* say about someone whose state is such that if all of the oceans of the world were full of the wine of Love, he would drink them all down and still shout about his thirst?" People imagine that Yahyā was speaking of intoxication and Bāyazid of sobriety. In fact, the reverse is true. The "possessor of sobriety" is the one who cannot bear even a single drop, while the "possessor of intoxication" is the one who drinks everything in his drunkenness and still needs more, drinking being the means to intoxication and things of the same kind being more proper to each other. Sobriety, however, is the opposite of drinking and cannot take ease with it.

Intoxication is of two kinds: one derives from the wine of benevolence, the other from the cup of Love. The intoxication of benevolence comes from secondary causes, since it is born from the vision of benefits. But the intoxication of Love has no cause, since it appears from the vision of the Benefactor. Hence, he who sees the benefit (i.e., the one intoxicated from benevolence) sees it in relation to himself, so he sees himself. But he who sees the Benefactor (i.e., the one intoxicated from Love) sees through Him and does not see himself. Even if he should be intoxicated, his intoxication is sobriety.

Sobriety is also of two kinds: sobriety because of heedlessness and sobriety because of Love. The sobriety of heedlessness is the greatest of veils, but the sobriety of Love is the most manifest unveiling. Hence, the sobriety that is joined to heedlessness is in reality intoxication, even if it is a kind of sobriety. Similarly, the sobriety that is joined to Love is truly sobriety, even if it is a kind of intoxication. When the Root is established, sobriety is like intoxication and intoxication like sobriety, but when the Root is not there, one could say the same thing.

In short, sobriety and intoxication upon the path of men are caused by diversity. When the Sultan of Reality shows His beauty, both sobriety and intoxication are seen as intruders since these two meanings are interconnected: the end of one is the beginning of the other. Beginning and end can only exist where there is separation. Since they are related to separation, they must be considered as equivalent to one another. As for Union, that is the negation of all separation. This is the significance of the verse:

When the morning dawns upon the star of wine,
the drunk and sober are shown to be equal.

There were once two masters in Sarakhs—Loqmān and Abol-Fazl Hasan. One day Loqmān came to visit Abol-Fazl and saw a book in his hand. He said, "O Abol-Fazl! What are you seeking in this book?"

Abol-Fazl replied, "The same thing that you are seeking by abandoning books!"

Loqmān said, "Then why is there this difference between us?"

Abol-Fazl answered, "It is you who see a difference, for you asked what I am seeking. Forget intoxication and become sober, then leave sobriety as well. Difference will disappear from your eyes and you will know what you and I are seeking."

DEFINITIONS OF INTOXICATION

1. Intoxication is the forgetfulness of those who have attained union.

2. The utmost limit of reason is bewilderment, and the utmost limit of bewilderment is intoxication.

3. Intoxication is the disappearance of phenomenal existence, the negation of habits, and the concealment of the object of knowledge.

4. Intoxication is that someone becomes absent from the ability to discern among things without becoming absent from things. (*Sharh-e ta'arrof*)

5. Intoxication is that the lover becomes absent within the Beloved, such that his sensory perception disappears and his breaths are consumed by fire. (*Mashrab al-arvāh*)

6. Intoxication is to speak about every hidden thing. (Hallāj, *Mashrab al-arvāh*)

7. Intoxication is the boiling of the heart when faced with the remembrance of the Beloved. (Abu 'Abdollāh ebn Khafif, *Mashrab al-arvāh*)

8. When the traces of things are effaced from the servant's innermost consciousness (*serr*), the coming of an influx of purity and light will not intoxicate him. But when contemplation and joyful expansion strike against him, their radiance will intoxicate him in relation to every influx that reaches him, and he who is intoxicated by description is veiled from Him who is described. (*Mashrab al-arvāh*)

DEFINITIONS OF SOBRIETY

1. Sobriety is for the heart to be cleansed of all that had veiled it from the Object of remembrance. (Ebn Khafif, *Mashrab al-arvāh*)

2. Sobriety is to maintain knowledge while contemplating God in intoxication and ecstasy. (*Mashrab al-arvāh*)

3. Those who have reached the Goal have gone through four stages: first unawareness, then bewilderment, then intoxication, and finally sobriety. These stages can be compared to the person who hears the name of the ocean, then comes near the ocean, then enters into the ocean, and finally is taken under by the waves. (Vāseti, *Mesbāh al-hedāyah*)

INTOXICATION ACCORDING TO THE MASTERS

Qoshayri writes:

Intoxication is to be absent from consciousness as the result of a powerful spiritual influx. Yet in one respect, intoxication is more than simple absence from consciousness (*ghaybat*), for its possessor may undergo a joyful expansion. If he is not completely overcome by the state of intoxication, the correct measure of things may leave his heart. This is the state of "semi-intoxication" (*tasākor*), where the spiritual influx is incomplete and sensory perception is still functioning. Sometimes the intoxication may go beyond the level of absence. It often happens that an intoxicated person's intoxication becomes so strong that he is in a greater state of absence than the one who is only in a state of absence. And it often happens that the possessor of absence has a more perfect absence than the possessor of intoxication, that is, if the latter is only semi-intoxicated rather than completely so. (*Resāla-ye qoshayriyah*)

Concerning the difference between intoxication and "absence from consciousness," Qoshayri writes:

> Absence may occur to God's servants as a result of the states that overcome their hearts (i.e., the various factors that cause desire and dread, or hope and fear). But intoxication belongs only to those who undergo spiritual ecstasy. Thus, when the Divine Beauty is unveiled to the servant, intoxication is the result, and his spirit is joyful and his heart enraptured. (*Resāla-ye qoshayriyah*)

Ansāri writes:

> God quotes Moses as follows: "He said, 'Oh God, show (Thyself) to me that I may gaze upon Thee'" (*Koran,* VII: 143). Intoxication is a term that alludes to the loss of self-control in ecstasy. It is one of the stations reserved for lovers, since the eyes of annihilation are not receptive to it and the degrees of knowledge cannot attain it.
>
> Intoxication has three signs: uneasiness at being occupied with transmitted reports while reverence is maintained, plunging into the fathomless depths of ecstatic desire while self-restraint is constant, and being drowned in the ocean of joy while patience is driven mad.
>
> Other than this is bewilderment, which has been called "intoxication out of ignorance," or rapturous love, which has been given the name "intoxication" improperly. Anything else derives from imperfection in vision, such as the intoxication of cupidity, or the intoxication of ignorance, or the intoxication of sensual passion. (*Manāzel as-sā'erin*)

'Ezzod-Din Kāshāni writes:

> In the terminology of the Sufis, the word "intox-

ication" refers to a lack of discernment between the properties of the outward (*zāher*) and the inward (*bāten*) due to the light of the intellect having been snatched away by the radiance of the light of God's Essence. This can be explained as follows. Those who undergo spiritual ecstasy are divided into two groups: the lovers of the Essence, whose ecstasy derives from the Essence, and the lovers of the Attributes, whose ecstasy derives from the world of the Divine Attributes.

In the ecstasy of the second group, many gaps and pauses intervene, in contrast to the ecstasy of the lovers of the Essence—this being due to the all-pervading nature of the Essence as opposed to the particular characteristics of the Attributes. Moreover, the ecstasy that derives from the world of the Attributes does not have the same strength as that which derives from the lights of the Essence.

Thus, at the beginning of his ecstasy, because of the strength and overpowering force of the influx, the Sufi whose ecstasy derives from the Essence is dominated by the power of his spiritual state. His intellect—which is his means of discernment and the vision of his heart—is snatched away and scattered by the constant recurrence and overpowering force of the rays of the Essence's lights. His discernment is removed from the hand of his own control and free choice. As a result, he cannot distinguish between the locus of the properties of the outward (i.e., dispersion) and the locus of the properties of the inward (i.e., gathering). He does not care if he divulges the mysteries of Lordship hidden within the treasury of the Divine Jealousy, and he displays his expansion with sayings like, "Glory be to Me" and "I am God." With respect to its recurrence and the strength of its overpowering force, this ecstasy is called a "state" (*hāl*), but with respect to the elimination of discernment it is called "intoxication." (*Mesbāh al-hedāyah*)

79

Ruzbahān writes as follows:

The lover reaches a state where he becomes purified of the dust of affliction and tribulation, contemplates the station of nearness, and gazes directly upon God with the eye of knowledge; the influxes of direct perception flow constantly into his heart as an effusion of the ever-increasing self-revelations of the Attributes and the incomparable Essence; the power of the influxes overcomes him such that he is shaken out of the domination of the station of his servanthood into the locus of proximity, and the unveiling of the Divine Beauty becomes too tremendous for the limits of his spiritual state. He becomes intoxicated with God: he is intoxicated with union through perception of perception. As much as his wine-drinking increases, his intoxication increases, until finally his spiritual "moment" is eternalized. Then, his intoxication is put upon a firm and stable basis.

Intoxication is only achieved by those who attain to sublime ecstasies, those to whom God unveils the lights of His Beauty. These lights bestow upon them joy, exhilaration, intoxication, absence, rapture and agitation. (*Mashrab al-arvāh*)

Kāshāni writes:

Just as "imitative ecstasy" (*tavājod*) is the first stage of ecstasy, so "imitative intoxication" (*tasākor*) is the first stage in intoxication. A sincere man who possesses imitative ecstasy is someone who experiences ecstasy without attaining the station of intoxication. Yet he is desirous and eager for the controlling power of a spiritual state to steal him away from dispersion in a single flash and drown him in gathering. Hence, the "imitative drunkard" is in ecstasy, the "drunkard" has been completely overcome by ec-

80

stasy, and the "sober" has been annihilated in His
Being. The first is often called a "possessor of tast-
ings," the second a "possessor of drinking," and third
a "possessor of quenched thirst." The flame of ecstasy
of the "taster" is soon snuffed out, like someone who
has only taken a sip of wine. The ecstasy of the
"drinker," however, receives successive and unabated
spiritual aid, so that the strength of his intellect is
overcome,' like one who consumes one cup of wine
after another and finally loses discernment.

In the words of Hāfez:

O you who know nothing
of our constant drinking,
We saw in the cup the reflection
of the face of the Friend.

'He whose thirst is quenched' experiences an ecstasy
so solidly entrenched and so powerful that he is un-
changed and unaffected by the constant flow of spiritual aid to his ecstasy. He is like a drinker who is so
addicted that the nature of the wine has become a
part of his éxistence. As much as he drinks, he does
not become drunk or lose discernment. (Adapted
from *Mesbāh al-hedāyah*)

SOBRIETY ACCORDING TO THE MASTERS

Kāshāni writes:

Sobriety is the returning of the faculty of discernment and the properties of gathering and dispersion
to their proper places. This can be explained as follows: After the traveler is finally annihilated and consumed by the overpowering lights of the Essence,

God bestows upon him a subsistent existence that is not naughted and destroyed by the radiance of the Essence's lights and returns to him every attribute that had been annihilated. Therefore intellect, which is the means of discernment, also returns, but it is now purified from the defilement of temporality, subsisting through God's subsistence. At this stage, the intellect becomes a partition between the spirit (*rūh*) and the soul (*nafs*), such that neither oversteps its own limits or infringes upon the sphere of the other. The intellect returns the property of gathering to its own domicile, which is the world of the spirit, and sends the property of dispersion back to its proper place, the world of the soul. Hence, orderliness of activity, refinement of speech, regard for proper customs and norms (*adab*), and concealment of the mysteries are all re-established such that they are safe from the bane of extinction. (*Mesbāh al-hedāyeh*)

Ansāri writes:

God says, ". . . When terror is lifted from their hearts, they will say, 'What said your Lord?' They will say, 'the Truth' " (*Koran*, XXXIV:23).

Sobriety is higher than intoxication and has an affinity with the station of expansion. It is a station beyond waiting, free of seeking, and purified of constriction—for a person only becomes intoxicated *with* God, but one is sober *in* God. Whatever is with God is not empty of bewilderment (not the bewilderment of doubt, but the bewilderment of the contemplation of the light of His Majesty). But whatever is *in* God is sound; it has no fear of imperfection, nor does it suffer any deficiency. Sobriety is one of the way-stations of the life of the spirit, one of the valleys of gathering, and one of the shining lights of direct perception. (*Manāzel as-sā'erin*)

According to Ruzbehān:

In the hearts of the lovers, the waves of Love's oceans calm down, the boiling of affection is subdued, and the tumult of desire becomes stilled. Then, the lovers attain to the Beloved in the station of intimacy. God reveals Himself to them while they contemplate Subsistence. In this station of Love, He holds back the lights of Tremendousness and Majesty from them, so they are overcome by the drunken states of intoxication. Hence, they perceive existence in the attributes of ease and intimacy, and they abide in the locus of union in a station of sobriety, which is unadulterated steadfastness and stability during the contemplation of proximity and the vision of Subsistence and Eternity-without-end. This station belongs to the perfect lovers, those who have reached the beginnings of the station of *tawhid*. Their intoxication and sobriety derive from a single source, which is the contemplation of the beauty of Eternity-without-beginning. (*Mashrab al-arvāh*)

This *faqir* (the author) says:

Intoxication and sobriety are spiritual states that cannot be earned or aquired. No person can choose one of them for himself, nor can he attain to one of them through his own effort. The Sufi submits himself to God's will. If God should bestow intoxication, that is pure kindness; and if He should bestow sobriety, that is unadulterated grace.

In the circle of Thy command,
*   we are the central point of submission.*
Kindness is whatever Thou shou'dst think,
*   our decision whatever Thou shou'dst command.*
*   Hāfez*

If everlasting form you desire,
find it in formlessness.
If knowledge of yourself you seek,
die to yourself and see yourself not.
'Attār

Annihilation and Subsistence

Sufi masters have discussed annihilation (*fanā'*) and subsistence (*baqā'*) extensively according to their own spiritual states and stations. Yet, for non-Sufis, this subject remains one of the more complex of those discussed in Sufism, and the great Sufis have made it even more difficult by expressing divergent views.

To the extent possible in words, this chapter will attempt to clarify the subject of annihilation and subsistence from the point of view of Sufism. The reader should be reminded, however, that *fanā'* and *baqā'* are spiritual states to be experienced, not topics to be discussed. Hence, words cannot explain this subject to the extent one might wish. Nevertheless, as Rumi says:

> *Though the ocean cannot be swallowed completely,*
> *taste it to the extent of your thirst!*

* * *

You, yourself, are veiling the way;
O Hafez, depart from the midst!
Content is he who travels this path
without a veil!

Hāfez

As a technical term in Sufism, the word annihilation
signifies the annihilation of the attributes of human nature
and their transformation into Divine Attributes. In the
state of annihilation, the Sufi is completely immersed in
the contemplation of the Attributes of God and oblivious
to his own self. Some masters have said that annihilation
means the annihilation of attributing acts to oneself, while
others have held that it means the annihilation of one's
vision of creation. It has also been said that annihilation
means the disappearance of the temporal in the face of the
first outpourings of the Eternal. In any case, annihilation
always proceeds from a lower stage to a higher stage, not
vice versa.

Baqā' or subsistence is the opposite of annihilation.
As a Sufi term, it signifies the traveler's gaining of subsistence through the Attributes of God after reaching annihilation. Those who reach this station become qualified by a
greater or lesser number of His Attributes.

In general, the wayfarer attains the station of subsistence in God according to different stations of annihilation: annihilation in His Essence (*dhāt*), in His Attributes
(*sefāt*), in His Acts (*af'āl*), and in His Effects (*āthār*), stations that are equivalent to the four levels of *tawhid* or the
"profession of Unity."

KINDS OF ANNIHILATION

Ebn 'Arabi has classified the kinds of annihilation as
follows:

1. Annihilation from breaking the *Shari'at* or Divine Law: This can be called "annihilation from sins."

2. Annihilation from acts: This is the stage of the traveler who has become annihilated from his own acts in the Acts of "He accomplishes what He desires" (*Koran,* XI:107). Such a Sufi contemplates God's Acts beyond the veils of created existence.

3. Annihilation from attributes: In this state, the Sufi is annihilated from created attributes. The possessor of this state is liberated from the bonds of unveiling and visions.

4. Annihilation from the essence: In this state, the Sufi realizes that his essence is composed of both a "subtle" (*latif*) and a "gross" (*kathif*) reality, the state of each being opposed to the other. His subtle reality has many and various forms, but his gross body is fixed within a single form, even though it undergoes variations in its accidental properties. If the Sufi becomes annihilated from his own essence in the Object of Contemplation, then in everyone who he contemplates he sees God as that person, and in every object of contemplation he sees God as that object. In this state of annihilation, if the contemplator should contemplate the subtle reality that is his own essence and see no others in himself, his annihilation is from himself in himself, for he is contemplating his own subtle reality, even if his body has been lost to sight. And if he should contemplate his bod in the state of this annihilation, his object of contemplation is his own fantasy; his state is like that of a sleeper who sees a dream.

5. Annihilation through the contemplation of God: If this kind of annihilation is actualized and the Sufi truly knows what he is seeing, he will have seen God with God's eye. But God does not become annihilated through the con-

templation of His own Essence, and the Sufi also will not be annihilated from the world in this state. His vision of the world will be through the direct vision of God, not through the vision of a being of the created worlds.

6. Annihilation from other than God through God: In this kind of annihilation, the Sufi does not contemplate separate entities. But if he contemplates God in His States, he has not been annihilated from everything other than God, and God remains forever in States. He says, "Every day He is in a state" (*Koran,* LV:29). If the Sufi should contemplate God's absolute Independence from the world, then he has reached the perfection of contemplation. God says, "Verily God is Independent of all beings" (*Koran,* III:97). It was in this station that Abu Bakr said, "I see nothing without seeing God before it." Likewise, in reference to such a station, the Prophet said, "God is, and nothing is with Him." In this station the Sufi contemplates the emanation of all things from God.

7. Annihilation from annihilation: Here there is a total absence of contemplation of annihilation. It can be compared to a dreamer in sleep who see images but does not know that he is asleep. The perfection of the drunkard is that he should be unaware of his intoxication. (Adapted from the *Rasā'el* of Shāh Ne'matollāh)

Concerning this last kind of annihilation, Jāmi writes:

"Annihilation" means that the overpowering force of the manifestation of God's Being to the Sufi's inward reality erases his awareness of other than God. It should be understood that "annihilation from annihilation" is contained in annihilation. That is, if the annihilated traveler is aware of his own annihilation, he is not truly annihilated, since both the attribute of annihilation and the possessor of that attribute are in

88

the category of "other than God." Hence, awareness of annihilation negates annihilation. (*Lavā'eh*)

Sohrawardi writes as follows:

When peace in the heart reaches its utmost limit, naturally the Sufi no longer looks at his own essence. His awareness of his own selfhood is nullified. This is called the "greatest annihilation." And when he forgets himself and forgets even his forgetfulness, this is called "annihilation within annihilation." (*Safir-e simorgh*)

Najmod-Din Kobrā writes:

Annihilation is of two kinds: annihilation of one's own attributes in God's Attributes (which is annihilation in Uniqueness) and annihilation of His Attributes in His Essence (which is annihilation in Oneness). When the Essence reveals Itself in theophany, It does so in the guise of Tremendousness. Hence, the traveler is demolished. He is on the point of death, but then he hears the words, "One! One!" When he is annihilated in His Essence, he subsists in Him and lives through Him.

THE DISTINCTION BETWEEN ANNIHILATION AND SUBSISTENCE

Subsistence in our view is nobler than annihilation. The one who has undergone annihilation regards the station of annihilation as lower than that of subsistence, and the one who experiences subsistence regards the station of subsistence as higher. Annihilation is our relationship to the world, while subsistence is our relationship to God. In subsistence God is contemplated, while in annihilation the creation is contemplated. Subsistence is an attribute of the substance, while annihilation is an attribute of the accident. (From the *Rasā'el* of Shāh Ne'matollāh)

THE MEANING OF ANNIHILATION

It should be pointed out here that annihilation does *not* mean that a person's reality ceases to exist, nor does it mean that one kind of existence is changed into another. Contrary to what certain people have imagined, annihilation does not entail a kind of suicide. On the contrary, it means the passing away of the human side of our nature in the Divine side. It should also be understood that the stage of annihilation does not come suddenly. Rather, with the first step that the traveler takes upon the path, he gradually moves forward on the way of annihilation. Moreover, the stage of subsistence begins at the same place. Each step the Sufi takes in departing from the human side of his nature is both a step toward annihilation and a step closer to subsistence, bringing him closer to the Divine. Rumi expressed this point well when he wrote:

> *The whole world has taken the wrong path from fear*
> *of non-existence, which in fact is its refuge.*
> *The non-existent one, who has gone outside himself,*
> *is the best and greatest of beings.*
> *In relation to God's Life he has been annihilated,*
> *but truly he has found subsistence in annihi-*
> *lation.*

It should also be kept in mind that since the annihilation of all human attributes is impossible, perfect annihilation cannot be achieved. The only exception to this is the

90

state of intoxication and selflessness, but even that is not perfect and continual in every respect.

THE PSYCHOLOGY OF ANNIHILATION AND SUBSISTENCE

> *When you polish and purify the mirror of your heart,*
> *you will see paintings beyond water and clay.*
> *Both paintings and Painter you will see,*
> *both the carpet of good fortune and the Carpet-spreader.*
>
> *Rumi*

At the beginning of the spiritual journey, in keeping with the *Koranic* verse, "Everything is perishing but His Face" (*Koran*, XXVIII:88), the Sufi holds that all that exists is God and that there is nothing and no one other than God. While traversing the stations of the path, he strives to experience this in practice. That is, he tries to grasp this truth directly in spiritual states, immediate perception, unveiling and contemplation, or to see it face to face with the eye of the heart. To accomplish this end, the Sufi strives to return to Infinity from which he had initially come. This return to Infinity can be likened to traveling the second half of a circle, the first half of which represents the journey from Infinity.

In Rumi's words:

> *Whoever remains far from his Origin*
> *strives to regain the days of his union with it.*

The *Koran* alludes to this return in a number of verses:

91

"... who reckon that they shall meet their Lord and that unto Him they are returning" (II:46).

"... who, when they are visited by an affliction, say, 'Surely we belong to God and to Him we return'" (II:156).

"All shall return to Us." (XXI:93)

"... that they are returning to their Lord." (XXIII:60).

At this point, one might ask what traversing the first half of this circle refers to. In order to describe this journey, we can say that the length of the first semi-circle extends from birth to maturity. In other words, man comes from another world (the womb) into this world. He grows, gains experience, and reaches maturity.

How then does he go about traversing the second half of the circle? The Sufis say that maturity is not sufficient. In order to reach spiritual maturity, man must travel the second semi-circle. He must go outside of the world of limitations, directions, intellect and discernment and forget "I and we" so that he can reach the world of Infinity and Eternity.

> *Since you are enclosed within the six directions,*
> *You seek Him there.*
> *But if your own directions become obliterated,*
> *You will see Him outside dimensions.*
> *Maghrebi*

Sufi masters have spoken vividly of these two kinds of maturity: "Ordinary maturity occurs when *mani* ("semen") leaves a man, but spiritual maturity occurs when man leaves *mani* ("I-ness")."

When an infant is first born, he does not perceive "I" and "you" and "he," but rather sees all things in one manner as a single entity. Gradually, the infant distinguishes himself from the things around him, seeing himself as a third person ("he"). Then, as a result of the experiences he undergoes and the things he learns from his parents and surroundings, he discerns and distinguishes his own self and turns his attention to "I." At this point, the child's "I" establishes relationships with his surroundings through his experiences of the outside world. He develops attachments and relationships within himself toward objects like his parents, family, teachers, people in authority, furnishings, wealth, position, self-regard, affection toward others, interest in a wife or husband, regard for self-subsistence, religion and God. These experiences of the outside world, as well as his earlier experiences, mix together with the individual's ego and gradually form the human personality. In this manner, sometime between the ages of 22 to 25 and in keeping with the difference between the sexes, the personality more or less becomes completed and brings into existence a world specific to the individual. Thus, he traverses the first semi-circle.

During its development, the child's "I" learns that certain experiences must be avoided, whereas others are allowed, and that certain natural desires should not be implemented. This learning brings into existence in the individual's mind a series of conflicts which each person faces in a particular manner. Sometimes, the individual succeeds in resolving his conflicts (i.e., becomes a healthy person); other times, however, he remains struggling with them (i.e., becomes unstable) and sometimes is defeated (i.e., becomes mentally ill).

PRELIMINARY REQUIREMENTS FOR TRAVERSING THE SECOND SEMI-CIRCLE

The first precondition for traversing the second semi-circle, or reaching spiritual maturity, is physical and mental health. If an individual has psychological problems, the master must first take him to the stage of total health (i.e., the master must be a "psychologist" for the disciple so that he can begin traversing the second semi-circle). This stage is called "preparation."

Certainly, the family environment has an effect upon the early development of the child and the forming of his ego and personality, so that if a child grows up in a family that might be called "incomplete" (i.e., in an environment devoid of love and mixed with conflict, struggle, and violence), his healthy development will be endangered. Similarly, at the beginning of the spiritual path a perfect master is needed, a guide who can help the disciple enter the spiritual life on a solid foundation. In this way, the disciple will be able to move forward on the "straight path" and be protected from deviation and error.

Imagine the traveler as an egg being formed into a bird under the wings of a dove. If the dove is not able to maintain the proper temperature and environment for the egg, it will rot and be prevented from reaching perfection (the stage of becoming a dove). In this analogy, the "Perfect Man" or master is like a bird who is able to maintain a variety of temperatures and environments under its wings for many different kinds of eggs. He is able to take different birds from the stage of an egg to the stage of a bird which flies in the air of God's Essence. But if the master is only a "good man" and not perfect, it is as if one were to place a duck egg under a chicken. It is possible that the duck will hatch from the egg, but it is certain that such a duck will not be able to follow all the details of the chicken's actions and will be left behind eventually. No one knows what the duck's destiny will be. This resembles those disciples in the history of Sufism who after a period of time have objected to their master, considered themselves higher than he, and separated their path from his.

ENTERING THE SECOND SEMI-CIRCLE

In order to reach spiritual perfection, man must relinquish, one by one and in reverse order (i.e., from last to first, or from new to old), everything that he has acquired from infancy to maturity. This is the meaning of the Prophet's saying, "Die before you die!"

One should know, however, that this return to simplicity is totally unrelated to the psychological disorder known as "regression" [1], for in every stage of his return the Sufi is self-conscious; his mental state and his relationship with his environment are maintained more harmoniously than before.

Regression is an unconscious flight from reality, while the Sufi's return is a conscious and willful movement toward God and Reality. While the traversing of the first semi-circle includes the perfecting of self-consciousness (which is necessary for mental maturity and the beginning of spiritual maturity), the second half of the circle is traversed solely for the sake of heart-consciousness, for which the rules and standards of the first semi-circle are not needed. The traveler on this way must be "free from everything that appears as an attachment" (Hāfez).

Various stages exist in the second half of the circle back to infinity:

1. As the Sufi enters the second semi-circle, which in reality is the journey back to God, he prepares himself to hope for nothing but God in order that he may reach the Truth. In this state, his *tawhid* ("profession of Unity") is expressed by the words, "Lā elāha ellallāh" ("There is no god but God"). That is, he wants nothing but God. He does not want anything that God does not love, and he loves that which God wants. He avoids bad attributes and

---

1. Freud was of the opinion that as soon as the child gains the ability to speak his first few words, he feels universal power in his own mouth; and as soon as he can move himself with his own hands and feet, he feels infinite power in his extremities. However, as he grows, he represses these feelings. Then in later years, when a person is faced with difficulties and becomes angry, he grinds his teeth, bites his lip, rubs his hands together, spits angrily, or curses. These are all regressions to that stage of infancy when the child felt infinite power in the parts of his body. In this way, he unconsciously tries to gain the help of that power.

strives to become qualified by God's Attributes. He turns away from the world of possible being and toward God, the Necessary Being. In this state the Sufi tramples upon his own wishes and desires. He eliminates all regard for the future from his consciousness, and replaces it with regard for God. Like Maghrebi, he asks:

> *O you who for a lifetime*
> *have desired union with Him,*
> *Why have you not passed beyond all desires*
> *for the sake of that desire?*

2. The second stage in attaining spiritual maturity is to eliminate all attachments to the past from the consciousness. The Sufi casts aside memories and past time and lives in the present, breaking his attachments to wife, husband, children, possessions, position, status, friends, knowledge, the talents of the particular intellect, and all other such things. In this connection, one must understand that most of these attachments derive from self-love in the sense that we love others so that they will love us, and we love things, position and knowledge so that they will protect us.

In this stage, the Sufi expresses his *tawhid* with the words, "Lā elāha ellā Anta". ("There is no god but Thou"). The tongue of his heart says, "Thou art worthy of my love. Until now I was attached to these things and cut off from Thee. Now I have chosen Thee and cut myself off from these attachments." Like Maghrebi, the Sufi says:

> *All at once, His all-encompassing Ocean*
> *plundered every created thing*
> *That Maghrebi had acquired.*

3. After cutting himself off from the past and the future, the Sufi's "I" remains without desire. In this state, the "I", which has placed its foot upon this world and the next, is

96

situated on the threshold of heart-awareness. The Sufi realizes that the expanse of the heart is in fact unlimited, since temporal things have no effect upon it; he sees everything as Eternal. Like Bāyazid he says, "Glory be to Me! How tremendous is My state!" Or like Hallāj he utters, "I am God." In this state, he expresses *tawhid* with the words, "Lā elāha ellā Anā" ("There is no god but I").

4. In the fourth stage, the Sufi pulls the veil of "I" to one side and places his foot upon his own head. He no longer speaks of "I", but only of "He". He becomes like Bāyazid in the following story:

One day someone came to -Bāyazid's door and knocked. The shaykh said, "Who are you seeking?"

The man replied, "Bāyazid."

Bāyazid then answered, "Poor Bāyazid! I have been seeking him for thirty years but have found no sign or trace of him."

In this state, the Sufi is like a child who has not yet learned the word "I," but calls everything by the third person. In the words of Sabzevāri:

> *O you who shout on the path of your search,*
> *"Friend! Friend!"*
> *In ka'aba or monastery, what is there other than*
> *Him?*
> *All is He, He!*

In this fourth stage of the journey, when the Sufi hears the Prophet's saying, "God was, and nothing was with Him," like Jonayd he says, "And He is now as He was."

Abu Sa'id Abol-Khayr once said:

I used to wander in the mountains and deserts entranced by the thought of reaching Him. Sometimes I found Him and sometimes I did not. But now

I have become such that I cannot find myself, for all is He and I am not, just as He was when I was not, and He will be when I will be not. (*Asrār at-tawhid*)

In reference to these words, 'Attār writes in the *Asrār-nāmah:*

> Listen to the words of the sultan of the Way,
>   the leader of religion, the king of the Truth,
> The Solomon who knows the spiritual bird's language,
> Abu Sa'id, the son of Abol-Khayr:
> "In every work and every state, for many long years
> I kept looking for His signs.
> When I found what I sought, I became lost
> like a drop drowned in the Sea.
> And now I am lost within the veil of mystery.
>   He who has lost himself finds himself not again."

5. In the preceding stage, perfect annihilation has still not been fully actualized, since the Sufi still sees an "other" who says "He." He must obliterate all expressions and allusions and become silent. This final stage is called "annihilation of annihilation," a stage alluded to in these words of the Prophet, "When the discussion comes to God, be silent!"

*   *   *

The masters have said, alluding to these stages, that:

> O son, the saints are the children of God!
> Whether they are present or absent,
> He knows full well their states.
>   *Rumi*

By means of these stages, the Sufi casts aside the veil of "other than God" or the central kernel of the turmoil of

98

life which veils Reality and causes his misfortunes and anxieties. He embraces the heart-embellishing Beloved who is pure felicity and true union. In this state, like a drop of water, the Sufi returns to the Ocean of Infinity and completes the circle of "We belong to God and to Him we return" (*Koran, II:156*). Like Maghrebi, once again, he becomes a nightingale:

> *Before the appearance of this cage of created beings,*
> *We all were nightingales within the garden of celes-*
> *tial secrets.*

Or, like Hāfez of Shirāz, he sings:

> *He whose heart has come alive through Love*
> *will never die.*
> *Our everlasting life is recorded*
> *in the ledger of the universe.*

SAYINGS OF THE MASTERS CONCERNING ANNIHILATION AND SUBSISTENCE

> *There is no veil between lover and Beloved,*
> *you are your own veil.*
> *O Hāfez, arise from in between!*
>
> *Hāfez*

In the "Conference of the Birds" (*Manteq at-Tayr*), 'Attār describes the valley of poverty and annihilation:

> *Next is the valley of poverty and annihilation:*
> *how is it possible to speak here?*
> *That valley is the same as forgetfulness,*
> *deafness, dumbness, and unconsciousness.*

You see a hundred thousand everlasting shadows
lost because of a single Sun!
When the universal Ocean decides to move,
how can the forms upon it stay in one place?
Both worlds are forms upon that Sea—nothing else;
whoever denies this is mad—nothing else.
When incense and firewood enter the fire,
both become ashes in the same place.
Both appear to you in the same form,
but in attributes the differences are great!

Rumi writes:

Someone said, "There is no darvish in the world,
and if there is, he is nonexistent."
He exists in respect to the subsistence
of his essence,
But his attributes have been naughted
in His Attributes.
Like the flame of a candle before the sun,
he is not;
But when you reflect, you see
that he is.
The candle's essence remains,
for if you place on it
A piece of cotton, it will burn
from the flames
But the candle is not, for annihilated
by the sun
It gives no illumination.

ANNIHILATION AND SUBSISTENCE ACCORDING TO HOJVIRI

"God says, 'What is with you comes to an end, but what is with God subsists' (*Koran*, XVI:96). And He says,

'All that dwells upon the earth is annihilated, but the face of thy Lord, the Majestic and Splendid, subsists' (*Koran,* LV:26-7).

"Know that 'annihilation' and 'subsistence' have one meaning in the language of the sciences, and another in the language of spiritual states. The exotericists are more bewildered by these expressions than by any other Sufi terms. In the language of the sciences and according to its etymology, 'subsistence' is of three kinds:

"First, a subsistence whose outset and end are in annihilation, like the subsistence of this world: at the beginning it did not exist, and at the end it will not exist, but it exists at the present moment.

"Second, a subsistence that did not exist and then came into existence, and which will never be annihilated. Such a subsistence belongs to heaven, hell, and the next world and its inhabitants.

"Third, a subsistence that never was not, and never will not be. This is God's subsistence and that of His Attributes—exalted be His Majesty for ever and ever! He and His Attributes are eternal. What is meant by His 'subsistence' is the everlastingness of His existence. Exalted is He above what the evildoers say! No one shares with Him in His Attributes.

"In the language of spiritual states, subsistence and annihilation may be expressed as follows. When ignorance is annihilated, necessarily knowledge subsists, and when disobedience is annihilated, obedience subsists, for the servant has actualized knowledge and obedience. In the same way, forgetfulness is annihilated through the subsistence of remembrance (*dhekr*). In other words, when the servant gains knowledge of God and subsists through knowledge of Him, he is annihilated from ignorance of Him. And when he is annihilated from forgetfulness, he subsists in His remembrance. This is the negation of blameworthy attributes through the establishment of praiseworthy ones.

"As for the elect of the Sufis, they have no need for the expressions we have mentioned on this subject. They do not speak of this matter in terms of 'sciences' and 'spiritual states', nor do they employ the terms 'annihilation' and 'subsistence' to refer to the stage of the perfection of the People of Sanctity—i.e., those who have been delivered from the toil of spiritual combat and freed from the shackle of stations and the alternation of states; who no longer seek but have found; who have seen with the eyes everything that can be seen, heard with the ears everything that can be heard, known with the heart everything that can be known, and found with the innermost consciousness everything that can be found; who in finding it have seen the ills of finding it; who have turned away from all things and whose intention has been annihilated within the Desire; who have traversed the Path, left aside claims, cut themselves off from meanings, seen miraculous works as veils, understood stations as stains, seen states in the guise of ills, remained without desires in their very Desire, abandoned all doctrines, and seen intimacy with all objects of intimacy as wasted, in accordance with God's words, 'That whosoever perished might perish by a clear sign and whosoever lived might live by a clear sign' (*Koran*, VIII:42).

"In reference to the meaning just expressed, I have composed this verse:

> *The annihilation of my annihilation*
> *is through the loss of my desire,*
> *For my desire in things*
> *has been transformed into Thy Desire.*

"When the servant becomes annihilated from his own attributes, he embraces subsistence totally. When the servant in the state of the existence of his attributes is annihilated from the ills of his attributes, he becomes subsistent in the subsistence of the Desire through the annihilation of desire. Thus, he has no proximity or distance, no alienation or intimacy, no sobriety or intoxication, no separation or union, no obliteration or eradication, no names or signs, no marks or imprints. In this connection one of the masters says:

My station and all phenomena have been swept away: I see neither·proximity nor distance in my moment's state. Through Him I have been annihilated from myself and the correct path has been made clear to me: This then is the purposeful Self-manifestation of God at the time of annihilation.

"In short, one cannot be annihilated from something without seeing its ills and negating one's desires for it. Whoever imagines that annihilation from something comes about through the veil of that thing is mistaken. It is not as if a person likes something and then says, 'I am subsistent through that'; nor is it as if as soon as he dislikes something he says, 'I am annihilated from that.' Both like and dislike are attributes of the seeker, but in annihilation neither remains, and in subsistence no distinctions are seen.

"A certain group have fallen into error in this regard. They imagine that annihilation means the loss of the essence and the naughting of the individual, and that subsistence means that God's subsistence becomes joined to the servant's. Both of these ideas are absurd. In India I saw a man who claimed knowledge of *Koranic* commentary, spiritual counsel, and the sciences. He debated with me concerning these matters. When I looked carefully, I saw that he did not understand annihilation and subsistence and could not discriminate between the Eternal and the temporal.

"There are many ignorant Sufis who consider the annihilation of man in his entirety permissible. We say to these mistaken and ignorant people, 'What do you mean by this annihilation?' If they say, 'annihilation of the entity,' that is absurd. But if they say, 'annihilation of the attributes,' then it is permissible for an attribute to be annihilated through the subsistence of another attribute, on the condition that both attributes are ascribed to the servant. But it is absurd for one person to be maintained by the attribute of someone else. . . .

"In short, whenever one thing becomes connected, joined, united and mixed with another, the properties of the two are as if the two were one. So our subsistence is our own attribute, and our annihilation is our own attribute. In the application of attributes to us, our annihilation is like our subsistence and vice versa. Hence, annihilation becomes an attribute through the subsistence of another attribute. Again, if someone should speak of an annihilation not related to a subsistence, that is permissible; similarly, to speak of a subsistence not related to an annihilation is also permissible—for what is meant by that annihilation is the remembrance of "others," and what is meant by that subsistence is the remembrance of God. Whoever is annihilated from his own desire gains subsistence in God's Desire, for your desire is annihilated while His Desire subsists. When you reside in your own desire, your desire will be annihilated, since you have resided in annihilation. But when you are controlled by God's Desire, His Desire subsists and you reside in subsistence.

"Metaphorically speaking, whatever falls under the domination of fire assumes fires attribute through its force, since the fire's domination transforms that thing's attributes. All the more so is this true of the domination of God's Will. Fire's domination transforms the attributes of the iron in the fire, while the iron's essence remains the same. Iron never becomes fire. And God knows best.

"In connection with this, each of the masters has pronounced subtle and symbolic allusions. Abu Sa'id Kharrāz, the founder of the school of annihilation and subsistence, says, 'Annihilation is the annihilation of the

104

servant from the vision of servanthood, and subsistence is the subsistence of the servant in contemplation of Divinity.' In other words, there are ills in the acts of servanthood, and the servant only reaches the reality of servanthood when he no longer looks at his own acts but is annihilated from the vision of self-activity and subsists in the vision of God's bounty. Here, all of his actions will be attributed to God, not to himself. All activity connected to the servant is imperfect, but everything that reaches him from God is perfect. Thus, when the servant is annihilated from what belongs to himself, he subsists in the beauty of God's Divinity.

"Abu Ya'qub Nahrajuri says, 'Correct servanthood lies in annihilation and subsistence.' The meaning here is that before the servant has left entirely his own portion, he will not be capable of sincere service. Hence, leaving the portion of humanity is annihilation, while sincerity in servanthood is subsistence.

"Ebrāhim Shaybān says, 'The science of annihilation and subsistence revolves around sincerity in Unity and correct servanthood. Everything other than this is sophistry and heresy.' In other words, when the servant acknowledges God's Unity, he sees himself overpowered and dominated by God's decree. He who is dominated is annihilated in the domination of the Dominator. When his annihilation becomes correct, he acknowledges his helplessness. He sees no remedy but servanthood and holds firmly to the threshold of contentment. If someone expresses annihilation and subsistence in a different manner (i.e., by calling annihilation the annihilation of the entity and subsistence the subsistence of the entity), that is pure heresy.

"All these things are close to one another with respect to their meaning, even if they differ in expression. The reality of all of them is that the servant is annihilated from his own existence through the vision of God's majesty and the unveiling of His tremendousness. In the overpowering force of His majesty, the servant forgets this world and the next; states and stations appear insignificant in his eyes; miraculous acts are obliterated from significance. He is annihilated from intellect and soul, even from annihilation. Within this very annihilation his tongue speaks through God, while his body is humble and abased. In the same way, when the seed first came forth from Adam's loins, the servant was in the state of the covenant of servanthood undefiled by any ills (cf. *Koran,* VII:172).

"In regard to this, one of the masters says:

> *When I know the way to Thee,*
> *I am not:*
> *Thou annihilated me from all, and I began*
> *to weep for Thee.*

"Another master says:

> *In my annihilation, my annihilation*
> *was annihilated,*
> *And in my annihilation,*
> *I found Thee.*
> *Thou obliterated my name and the trace*
> *of my body;*
> *I was asked about myself*
> *and said 'Thou.' "*
> (from the *Kashf al-mahjub*)

*   *   *

Hojviri also writes:
"One day I was with Khājah Abu Ahmad Mozaffar ebn Ahmad. One of the pretenders of Nishapur was with him, and among other things he said, 'A person becomes annihilated after attaining subsistence.' Khājah Mozaffar said, 'How can annihilation take place in subsistence? Annihilation consists of nonexistence, whereas subsistence refers to existence. Each of these negates its companion (i.e.,

106

its opposite), so the meaning of annihilation is obvious. But if something that was nonexistent becomes existent, it is not the same entity, but something else. It is not admissible for essences to become annihilated, yet the annihilation of attributes and secondary causes is admissible. Hence, when attributes and secondary causes become annihilated, the possessor of the attributes and the causer remain. The annihilation of his essence is not admissible.'

"I do not remember the exact words of that master, but the purport of his words was as I have mentioned. Let me explain what he meant, so that his words may be applied more generally. The servant's free-will is his own attribute, and the servant is veiled by his own free-will from God's free-will. Hence, the servant's attribute veils him from God. Inevitably, God's free-will is eternal, while the servant's free-will is temporal. The eternal cannot be annihilated. Thus, when God's free-will becomes subsistent for the servant, necessarily his own free-will is annihilated and his self-activity ceases. And God knows best." (*Kashf al-mahjub*)

ANNIHILATION AND SUBSISTENCE ACCORDING TO 'EZZOD-DIN KĀSHĀNI

"Annihilation is the end of the journey *to* God, while subsistence is the beginning of the journey *in* God—for the journey to God comes to an end when the traveler traverses totally the desert of existence on the feet of sincerity, while the journey *in* God becomes actualized when, after absolute annihilation, the servant is given an existence and essence cleansed from the stain of temporality. By means of this existence and essence, he ascends within the world of becoming qualified by the Divine Attributes and acquiring the Divine Traits.

"The discrepancies among the words of the masters in defining annihilation and subsistence derive from the discrepancies among the words of the questioners. The masters have answered each person in keeping with his understanding and best interest. They have seldom spoken of *absolute* annihilation and subsistence because of the grandeur of these two states.

"Some have said that what is meant by annihilation is the annihilation of all acts opposed to the *Shari'at* and by subsistence the subsistence of acts in conformity with it. This understanding of the terms derives from sincere repentance.

"Others have said that annihilation is the disappearance of the pleasures of the world, as indicated in the saying, 'It makes no difference to me whether I see a woman or a wall.' In this sense, subsistence is subsistence of the desire for the next world. This understanding derives from the station of asceticism.

"Others have said that annihilation is the disappearance of the pleasures of both this world and the next, and that subsistence is the subsistence of desire for God. Thus Abu Sa'id Kharrāz says, 'The mark of the one who claims annihilation is that his joy in this world and the next departs, leaving only joy in God.' This understanding derives from a true realization of 'essential Love' (*mahabbat-e dhāti*).

"Another group have said that annihilation is the annihilation of blameworthy attributes, and subsistence is the subsistence of beautiful attributes. This understanding is a result of purification and the adornment of the soul.

"Still others have said that annihilation is absence from things, and subsistence is presence with God. This understanding results from the intoxication of spiritual states.

"Shaykh al-Islām Sohrawardi says, 'Absolute annihilation is that God's command overwhelms the servant, so that God's Being overwhelms his being.' This is the reality of absolute annihilation, whereas the other types constitute annihilation only in certain respects.

"Annihilation is of two kinds: annihilation of the outward and annihilation of the inward. Annihilation of the outward is the annihilation of man's actions and their results in the theophany of the Divine Acts. The possessor of this kind of annihilation is drowned in the ocean of Divine Acts to the extent that he sees himself and every other created being as possessing no acts, will, or free choice. He affirms nothing but the Acts, Will, and Free Choice of God. His power of choice is taken completely away from him, so that he has no power to choose or undertake any act himself. He enjoys the contemplation of the unaccompanied Act of God without the stain of the acts of others. Some of the travelers have remained in this state without eating or drinking until God appointed someone to take care of them, and provide them with food, drink and other necessities.

" 'Annihilation of the inward' refers to the annihilation of attributes and the annihilation of the essence. The possessor of this state is sometimes drowned in the annihilation of his own attributes through the unveiling of the eternal Attributes, and sometimes drowned in the annihilation of his own essence through the contemplation of the traces of the tremendousness of the eternal Essence. God's Being overcomes and dominates him to the extent that his inwardness is annihilated from all intruding ideas and thoughts.

"Shaykh al-Islām relates the following story in this regard: 'Once I asked Abu Mohammad 'Abdollāh Basri, "Is the subsistence of images within the innermost consciousness and the existence of intruding thoughts a kind of hidden idolatry?" I had always held that such was the case, but Basri replied, "This is only so in the station of annihilation.' "

What is meant here—and God knows best—is that the subsistence of such thoughts for someone who has not yet passed beyond the station of annihilation is idolatry, but not for someone who has attained subsistence after annihilation.

"As for the absence from sensation, that is not a necessary concomitant of the station of annihilation. Rather, it may occur for some people and not for others. Metaphorically speaking, the reason that someone may not become absent from sensation lies in the expanse of the container: both annihilation and presence may be contained within it. The traveler's inward reality is drowned in the depths of annihilation, while his outward reality is present with everything that is said or occurs. This may take place when he has become firmly established in the station of the contemplation of the Essence of the Attributes and has returned to sobriety from the intoxication resulting from the state of annihilation. But he who is still at the beginning of this state is made absent from sensation by his intoxication. Thus, for example, 'Abdollāh ebn 'Omar was once circumambulating the ka'aba. A person greeted him, but he did not hear and failed to return the greeting. Later that person reproached him for this. 'Abdollāh replied, 'In that place I was beholding God.' It has also been reported that Moslem ebn Yasār was once praying in the congregational mosque in Basra when all at once a pillar fell over. It made so much noise that all the people in the bazaar heard it, yet Ebn Yasār, within the mosque, was unaware of it.

"The subsistence corresponding to the annihilation of the outward is that God makes the servant, after the annihilation of free-will and choice, the possessor of His free-will and choice. God loosens the reins of his control over affairs so that he may do whatever he wants through God's free-will and choice. Just as the one who abandons free-will absolutely resides in one of the levels of annihilation, so too does the one who abandons free-will in general, referring individual matters to God inwardly, until God gives him permission to employ free-will.

"The subsistence corresponding to the annihilation of the inward is that the annihilated essence and attributes are resurrected from the grave of concealment into the gathering place of manifestation, and the veil is totally lifted, so that God is not the veil of creatures, nor are the

110

creatures the veil of God. The possessor of annihilation is veiled from the creatures by God, just as he who has not reached the station of annihilation is veiled from God by the creatures. But the possessor of subsistence after annihilation contemplates each in its own station without one becoming the veil of the other. In him, annihilation and subsistence are joined and intertwined. In annihilation he is subsistent, and in subsistence he is annihilated. However, in the state where subsistence is manifested, annihilation is contained within him by way of knowledge, while in the state where annihilation is manifested, subsistence is embraced in knowledge. Thus, Abu Sa'id Kharrāz has said, 'The correct state of the People of Annihilation in annihilation is that they possess the knowledge of subsistence, and the correct state of the People of Subsistence in subsistence is that they possess the knowledge of annihilation.' He also said, 'Annihilation is to be naughted by God, while subsistence is to be present with Him.' Jonayd says, 'Annihilation is that you become totally ignorant of your own attributes and totally occupied with His Totality.' This statement embraces all of the dimensions of recognizing the annihilation of both the outward and the inward.

"The annihilation of the outward is the share of the Possessors of Hearts and States, while the annihilation of the inward is the exclusive possession of God's Free Ones who have been delivered from the bondage of being controlled by states and who come out from under the veil of the heart. They have abandoned the companionship of the heart for that of 'Him who turns the heart wherever He wills.' " (*Mesbāh al-hedāyah*)

ANNIHILATION AND SUBSISTENCE ACCORDING TO ANSĀRI

"God says, 'All that dwells upon the earth is annihilated, but the Face of thy Lord subsists' (*Koran*, LV:26-7).

In this context, annihilation is the dissolution of everything other than God: through theory, then through rejection, then in truth. It contains three degrees:

"The first degree is the annihilation of knowledge within the Known, which is annihilation through theory; the annihilation of direct vision in the Seen, which is annihilation through rejection; and the annihilation of seeking through finding, which is annihilation in truth.

"The second degree is the annihilation of the contemplation of seeking until its overthrow, the annihilation of the contemplation of knowledge until its overthrow, and the annihilation of the contemplation of direct vision until its overthrow.

"The third degree is the annihilation from the contemplation of annihilation. This is true annihilation. It observes the lightning flash of vision, journeys upon the sea of gathering, and travels on the way of subsistence.

"God says, 'God is better and more subsistent' (*Koran*, XX:73). Subsistence is a term for what remains standing after the annihilation and overthrow of all contemplated things. It has three degrees: the first is the subsistence of the Known after the overthrow of knowledge—in actuality, not in theory. The second is the subsistence of the Contemplated after the overthrow of contemplation—ontologically, not just in description. The third is the subsistence of what exists eternally—in truth, through the overthrow of that which is not, by obliterating it." (*Manāzel as-sā'erin*)

Ansāri also writes as follows:

"The ninety-ninth battlefield is annihilation. God says, 'All things are perishing except His Face. His is the judgement, and unto Him you shall be returned' (XXVIII:88). Annihilation is naughting, and this naughting takes place through three things in three things: the naughting of finding in the Found, the naughting of knowledge in the Known, and the naughting of vision in the Seen. What can 'that-which-is-not' find within 'That-

Which-Ever-Was?" How can subsistent God become joined to the phenomenal being in annihilation? How can the Worthy be united with the unworthy?

"Everything other than He is in the midst of three things: yesterday's nonexistence, today's lostness, and tomorrow's naughtedness. Thus, all are nonexistent except for Him, yet existent through Him. Thus all are His Existence. When the rain reaches the sea it attains completion. The star disappears in daylight. He who reaches the Lord attains to Self.

"The one hundredth battlefield is subsistence. God says, 'God is better and more subsistent' (*Koran,* XX:73). God—nothing else: attachments severed, secondary causes dissolved, appearances nullified, limitations naughted, understandings annihilated, history absurd, allusions blind, expressions negated, harm obliterated, and God the One subsists through His own Selfhood." (*Sad maydān*)

ANNIHILATION AND SUBSISTENCE ACCORDING TO QOSHAYRI

"Annihilation is to be purified from blameworthy attributes, while subsistence is the acquisition of praiseworthy attributes. Whoever sees that all activity and laws are in His power is said to have become annihilated from Time's revolution and from creation. When he becomes annihilated from imagining that the traces which are the creatures have existence, and he comes to know that they have nothing, he becomes subsistent through God's Attributes. Whoever is overcome by the dominating power of Reality so that he sees nothing of 'others,' neither entity nor trace, is said to have become annihilated from the creatures and subsistent in God.

"The annihilation of the servant from his blameworthy and contemptible states and acts is their nonexistence, while his annihilation from himself and the creatures is

113

that he has no sensation of himself or of them. When he becomes annihilated from states, acts and traits, it is not permissible that any of these things become existent. But when it is said, 'He became annihilated from himself and the creatures,' his self and the creatures still exist. However, he has no knowledge, sensation, or awareness of them. That is, his self exists and the creatures exist, but he is unaware and unconscious of both himself and the creatures." (*Resāla-ye qoshayriyah*)

It is fitting to conclude this chapter with the following poem of Shamsod-Din Maghrebi which expresses beautifully the state of annihilation:

> *How can Time know my name and trace? Who but the Friend*
> > *could know my essence and attribute?*
> *When someone's existence has been concealed by God,*
> > *how can he be known by any but Him?*
> *I who am lost in Thee—how could anyone find me?*
> > *Who on the shore knows the one drowned in Thy Sea?*
> *I who am not light—how should the Men of Light know me?*
> > *I who am not fire—how should the men of Fire know me?*
> *Since I have packed my bags and left both worlds,*
> > *how can I be considered one of those who must settle accounts on the Day of Resurrection?*
> *I who have lost my being in Thee—no being knows me.*
> > *I am drunk in Thee—how could a sober man know me?*
> *Speak not of the many before me who has seen the One.*
> > *How can he who has seen only the One know the many?*

He who is shackled by heart, spirit, intellect, and
   soul—
   how could he know me, me who has escaped
   from all four?
How can the one imprisoned in the dungeon of created being
   have news of Maghrebi, who has fled the dungeon? How?

APPENDIX

What follows below is a compendium of the persons and books mentioned in the text. It should be noted that very little information is provided about certain figures since they are practically unknown with the exception of one or two quotations from them in classical texts. For reference purposes, at least one source (English, Persian or Arabic) has usually been provided for each person mentioned. The following abbreviations have been employed:

KM. *The Kashf al-Mahjub. The Oldest Persian Treatise on Sufism,* by al-Hujwiri, translated by R.A. Nicholson, London, 1911, reprinted 1970.

MP. *Masters of the Path: A History of the Masters of the Nimatullahi Sufi Order,* by Dr. Javad Nurbakhsh, New York, 1980.

MSM. *Muslim Saints and Mystics, Episodes from the Tadhkirat al-awliyā',* translated by A. J. Arberry, Chicago, 1966.

NF. *Nafahāt al-ons* by Jāmi, ed. by M. Tawhidipur, Tehran, 1336/1957.

TA. *Tadhkerat al-awliyā'* by 'Attār, ed. by M. Este'lāmi, Tehran, 1346/1967.

TS. *Tabaqāt as-sufiyah* by Solami, ed. by Nur ad-Din Sharibah, Cairo, 1372/1953.

'Abdollāh ebn Khobayq, Abu Mohammad Antāki: A Sufi of the third/ninth century. KM 128.

'Abdollāh ebn 'Omar (d. 73/692): The son of the second caliph and a companion of the Prophet, he transmitted over 2000 of the Prophet's sayings. In Hojviri's words, he was one of the "People of the Veranda." KM 81.

Abhari, Abu Bakr ebn Tāher (d. c. 330/942): A companion of Shebli. TS 391.

Abol-'Abbās Sayyāri: The founder of one of the twelve Sufi orders listed by Hojviri (KM 251), he lived in the third/ninth century. KM 157.

Abol-Fazl Hasan (second half of fourth/tenth century): He was the master of Abu Sa'id Abol-Khayr. TA 816.

Abol-Hasan Hosri (d. 371/981-2): A disciple of Shebli, he lived in Baghdad. KM 160.

Abol-Hosayn Nuri (d. 295/908): One of the more famous of the early masters. KM 130, MSM 221.

Abol-Qāsem Fāres of Baghdad (third/ninth century): A disciple of Hallāj. NF 154.

Abol-Qāsem Hakim, Eshāq ebn Mohammad (d. 342/953): He is known more as a jurisprudent and theologian than as a Sufi.

Abol-Qāsem Jonayd (d. 298/910): One of the most famous of the Sufi masters and the head of the "Baghdad School." KM 128, MP 20, MSM 199.

Abu 'Abdollāh ebn Khafif (d. 371/982): A famous master from Shiraz, he is the author of a number of books, KM 158, MSM 257.

Abu 'Ali Daqqāq (d. 405/1014-15 or 412/1021-2): This famous master was learned in many sciences. KM 162.

Abu 'Ali Jawzjāni, Hasan ebn 'Ali (d. early fourth/tenth century): A master from Khorasan. KM 147.

Abu 'Ali Rudbāri (d. 322 or 323/943-5): One of the great masters and companion of Jonayd, Nuri, and Ebn Jalā', KM 157, MP 23.

Abu 'Amr Demashqi (d. 320/932): A companion of Dhon-Nun and Ebn Jalā'. TS 277.

Abu Bakr Qahtabi (or Qahti) (fourth/tenth century):

Nothing seems to be known about him except the anecdote related by Qoshayri.

Abu Bakr Shebli (d. 334/946): A companion of Jonayd and one of the outstanding figures of the Baghdad circle of Sufism. KM 155, MSM 277.

Abu Bakr Vāseti, Mohammad ebn Musā (d. after 320/932): According to 'Attār, he was the greatest master of his time; one of the earliest disciples of Jonayd. KM 154.

Abu Hafs Haddād Nayshāburi (d. 265/879): A blacksmith who became one of the famous masters of Khorasan. KM 123, MSM 192.

Abu Mohammad ebn 'Abdollāh Basri (sixth/twelfth century): One of the masters of Shehābod-Din 'Omar Sohravardi.

Abu Mohammad Jorayri (d. 311/923-4): One of Jonayd's greatest disciples. TA 579.

Abu Nasr Sarrāj (d. 378/988): The author of al-Loma' (q.v.), he met many of the great masters, such as Sari and Sahl. TA 639.

Abu 'Othmān Hiri (d. 298/911): A companion of Shāh ebn Shojā' and Yahyā ebn Mo'ādh. KM 132, MSM 231.

Abu 'Othmān Maghrebi (d. 373/983-4): See MP 26, KM 158.

Abu Sa'id Abol-Khayr (d. 440/1049): One of the most famous early masters, especially because of his biography, Asrār at-tawhid (q.v.). See Nicholson, Studies in Islamic Mysticism, Cambridge, 1921, ch.1.

Abu Sa'id Kharrāz (d. 286/899): A companion of Dhon-Nun and Sari, he is said to have been the first to use the terms annihilation and subsistence. KM 143, MSM 218.

Abu Sa'id Qorashi: He seems to be unknown except for a few references to him by Ruzbehān in Mashrab al-arvāh.

Abu Solaymān Dārāni (in some sources, Dārā'i) (d. 205/ 820): One of the famous early masters. KM 112.

Abu Ya'qub Nahrajuri (d. 330/941-2): A companion of 'Amr ebn 'Othmān and Jonayd. TA 506.

Ahmad ebn 'Āsem Antāki (third/ninth century): A disciple of Mohāsebi and companion of Beshr, Sari and Fozayl. KM 127.

'Amr ebn 'Othmān Makki (d. 291/904): A disciple of Jonayd. KM 138, MSM 214.

Ansāri, Khwājah 'Abdollāh, known as Shaykh al-Islam and the Pir of Herat (d. 481/1088): A master who wrote such well-known works as the *Monājāt* ("Intimate Conversations"—translated into English at least twice), *Tabaqāt as-sufiyah* (q.v.) and *Manāzel as-sā'erin* (q.v.).

Asrār at-tawhid (The Mysteries of Tawhid): A biography of Abu Sa'id Abol-Khayr, written by his great-great-grandson in beautiful and simple Persian.

Asrār-nāmah (The Book of Mysteries): One of 'Attār's long didactic poems.

'Attār (d. 618/1221): A famous Persian Sufi poet, author of such works as *Asrār-nāmah* and *Manteq at-tayr.*

'Avāref al-ma'āref (Gifts of Knowledge): A classic textbook of Sufi theory and practice written by Shehāb ad-Din 'Omar Sohravardi (q.v.). See *Mesbāh el-hedāyah.*

Bābā Tāher Hamadāni (d. 410/1019-20): A Sufi famous for his poems in a Persian dialect and for his Arabic aphorisms.

Bāyazid Bastāmi (d. 261/874 or 264/877): One of the most famous of all Sufis, known especially for his "ecstatic" utterances. KM 106, MSM 100.

Beshr Hāfi (d. 227/841-2): Besides being a Sufi, he was an authority on *Hadith.* KM 105, MSM 80.

Bondār ebn al-Hosayn as-Sufi (d. 353/964): A disciple of Shebli. TX 467.

Dhon-Nun Mesri (d. 246/861): A famous early Sufi from Egypt who is said to have known the occult sciences and the secret of the Egyptian hieroglyphs. MSM 87.

Ebn 'Arabi (d. 638/1240): The famous Andalusian Sufi whose metaphysical expositions have deeply influenced the presentation of Sufi teachings from his own time to the present day. Shāh Ne'matollāh among others devoted many of his prose works to translating Ebn 'Arabi's works into Persian and explaining them.

Ebn 'Atā', Abol-'Abbās (d. 309/922): A close companion of Jonayd. MSM 236.

Ebn Jalā', Abu 'Abdollāh Ahmad ebn Mohammad (d. 306/918): He met Dhon-Nun and was a companion of Jonayd and Nuri. KM 134.

Ebn Khafif: See Abu 'Abdollāh ebn Khafif.

Ebrāhim ebn Shaybān (d. 377/948-9): A disciple of two well-known masters, Ebrāhim Khavvās and Abu 'Abdollāh Maghrebi. TA 717.

Ehyā' 'olum ad-din (The Revivification of the Sciences of Religion): The famous masterpiece of Ghazzāli, (q.v.), many sections of which have been translated into English.

'Elal al-maqāmāt (The Defects of the Stations): A short Arabic work by Ansāri describing the dangers facing the spiritual traveler in each of the stations of the path. The work has been translated into French.

'Ezzod-Din Kāshāni (d. 735/1334-5): A member of the Sohravardiyah order, he wrote the *Mesbāh al-hedāyah* and other important works.

'Erāqi, Fakhrod-Din (d. 688/1289): A follower of Ebn 'Arabi, he is the author of a *divān* of Persian poetry, but his fame rests mainly on his prose masterpiece, the *Lama'āt*, a Persian summary of Ebn 'Arabi's teachings in the language of Love.

Estelāh as-sufiyah (The Technical Terms of the Sufis): A very brief work by Ebn 'Arabi defining a few Sufi terms.

Fozayl ebn 'Eyāz (d. 187/803): A famous early ascetic and Sufi. KM 97, MSM 52.

Ghazzāli (d. 505/1111): A Sufi and theologian who wrote numerous works and is famous for giving Sufism a more respected position among the doctors of the *Shari'at*. Numerous studies of him have been written in European languages.

Golshan-e rāz (The Rosegarden of Mystery): A Persian poem by Shabestari of about 1000 verses summarizing the teachings of Ebn 'Arabi. It has been partly or wholly translated into English a number of times.

Hāfez (d. 792/1390): One of the most famous and beloved of the Persian Sufi poets. Many have attempted to translate his poetry into English, but with little success.

Hallāj (d. 309/922): The famous martyr and archetypal intoxicated lover of God. KM 150, MSM 264.

Hāreth Mohāsebi (d. 243/857): One of the most important early Sufi authors. KM 108, MSM 143.

Hātem Asamm (d. 237/852): A well-known early Sufi. KM 115, MSM 150.

Hojviri (d. 465/1072-3): The author of *Kashf al-mahjub*.

Hosri: See Abol-Hasan.

Jāmi (d. 898/1492): A famous Persian Sufi poet, he was also the author of many prose works in both Arabic and Persian. He had considerable influence in spreading the teachings of Ebn 'Arabi.

Jonayd: See Abol-Qāsem.

Kashf al-mahjub (The Unveiling of the Veiled): A classic Persian text on Sufism by Hojviri, translated into English from an incomplete manuscript by Nicholson. KM.

Kholāsa-ye sharh-e ta'arrof (The Summary of Sharh-e

Ta'arrof): An eighth/fourteenth century summary of the *Sharh-e ta'arrof* (q.v.) which drops most of the long anecdotes and explanations.

Lavā'eh (Flashes): A beautiful Persian summary of Ebn 'Arabi's teachings by Jāmi, translated into English by Whinfield.

Al-Loma' (Gleams): One of the earliest Arabic textbooks on Sufi teaching and practice, by Abu Nasr Sarrāj. Edited and abstracted by Nicholson (*The Kitab al-Loma'*, London, 1914).

Loqmān (al-Hakim): A pre-Islamic wise man mentioned in the Koran.

Loqmān: A figure whose name has been preserved largely because of the anecdotes related about him and Abol-Fazl Hasan (q.v.).

Maghrebi, Shamsod-Din (d. 809/1406-7): A well-known Persian Sufi poet and follower of Ebn 'Arabi's school. See also Abu 'Othmān.

Mālek ebn Dinār (d. c. 130/748): A disciple of Hasan of Basra. KM 89, MSM 26.

Manāzel as-sā'erin (The Waystations of the Travelers) by Ansāri: An Arabic description of 100 spiritual stations which the Sufis traverse in their journey to God. The work has been translated into French.

Manteq at-tayr (The Language of the Birds): 'Attār's famous Persian didactic poem. It has been translated into English.

Mashrab 'al-arvāh (The Drinking-place of the Spirits): An Arabic work by Ruzbehān describing 1000 spiritual stations.

Mathnavi (Couplets): Rumi's famous didactic poem, translated into English in three volumes by Nicholson.

Maybodi, Rashid ad-Din (sixth/twelfth century): The author of a famous Persian commentary on the Koran. See *Tafsir*.

Mesbāh al-hedāyah (The Lamp of Guidance): A Persian revision of the *'Avāref al-ma'āref* (q.v.) by 'Ezzoddin Kāshāni, and a classic Sufi textbook. It was partially translated into English by Wilberforce Clarke as *The 'Awarifu-l-ma'ārif* (Calcutta, 1891; N.Y., 1970).

Mohammad ebn 'Aliyān (third/ninth century): A companion of Abu 'Othmān Hiri. TS 417.

Mohammad ebn Fazl, Abu 'Abdollah (d. 319/931): A great master from Balkh. KM 140.

Mohāsebi: See Hāreth.

Moslem ebn Yasār (d. 100/718 or 101/719): A well-known ascetic.

Motarref ebn 'Abdollāh ebn ash-Shekhir (d. 95/713-4): Little is known about him save a few sayings attributed to him.

Mozaffar, Abu Ahmad ebn Ahmad: Apparently unknown except for Hojviri's mention of him.

Mozayyen, Abol-Hasan 'Ali ebn Mohammad (d. 328/939-40): A companion of Sahl and Jonayd. TS 382.

Najmod-Din Kobrā (d. 618/1221): Founder of one of the major Sufi orders, the Kobraviyah.

Nuri: See Abol-Hosayn.

Qoshayri, Abol-Qāsem (d. 465/1072-3): A disciple of Abu 'Ali Daqqāq and a master in his own turn, he is the author of several works, the most famous being his *Resālah* (q.v.). KM 167.

Rasā'el (Treatises) of Ansāri: One of Ansāri's long Persian works, consisting of a collection of sayings and anecdotes on Sufi ethics and practice.

Rasā'el (Treatises) of Shāh Ne'matollāh: The collected prose work of Shāh Ne'matollāh, edited and published by Dr. Nurbakhsh. Four of a projected six volumes have appeared.

Resāla-ye qoshayriyah (The Treatise of Qoshayri): One of the most famous and authoritative early works on Sufism, in Arabic, by Abol-Qāsem Qoshayri. An early Persian translation is extant.

Rumi (d. 672/1273): One of the greatest Persian Sufi poets and the most translated.

Ruzbehān Baqli (d. 606/1209-10): A famous Sufi from Shiraz, author of many works in Arabic and Persian.

Sabzevāri, Hājj Mollā Hādi (d. 1289/1873): The most famous Iranian philosopher and sage of the nineteenth century.

Sa'di (d. between 691/1292 and 695/1296): A Persian Sufi poet most famous for his *Golestān*, probably the greatest prose work of the Persian language.

Sad Maydan (One Hundred Battlefields): A Persian discussion of the spiritual stations by Ansāri.

Safir-e simorgh (The Call of the Phoenix): A short Sufi treatise in exquisite Persian by Sohravardi the philosopher.

Sahl ebn 'Abdollāh Tostari (d. 282/896): A well-known master, his master was Sofyān Thawri. KM 139, MSM 153.

Sari Saqati (d. 251/865 or 253/867): A famous master and uncle of Jonayd. KM 110, MP 19, MSM 166.

Shabestari, Mahmud (d. 720/1320): Author of the *Golshan-e rāz* (q.v.) and a number of short prose works in Persian.

Shāh ebn Shojā' Kermāni (d. after 270/884): Of royal blood, he saw many of the great masters of his day, including Yahyā ebn Mo'ādh, and is the author of a number of books on Sufism. KM 138, MSM 183.

Shāh Ne'matollāh Vali (d. 832/1429 or 834/1431): The master for whom the Nimatullahi Order is named. MP 39.

Shāh Qāsem Anvār (d. 837/1433): A Persian Sufi poet, disciple of Safiyod-Din Ardabili and companion of Shāh Ne'matollāh.

Sharh-e kalemāt-e qesār-e Bābā Tāher (Commentary on the Aphorisms of Bābā Tāher): An Arabic work by the well-known Sufi 'Ayn al-Qozāt Hamadāni (d. 525/1131).

Sharh-e ta'arrof (Commentary on at-Ta'arrof) by Abu Ebrāhim Mostamli Bokhāri (d. 434/1042-3): One of the earliest Persian works on Sufism, it is a long commentary on the Arabic *at-Ta'arrof* by Abu Bakr al-Kalābādhi. The latter work was translated by Arberry as *The Doctrine of the Sufis.*

Shebli: See Abu Bakr.

Sohravardi, Shaykh al-Islam Shehābod-Din 'Omar (d. 632/1234-5): The founder of the Sohravardi Order, master of such figures as Sa'di and Awhadod-Din Kermāni, and author of *'Avāref al-ma'āref* (q.v.).

Sohravardi, Shehābod-Din Yahyā (d. 587/1191): A Sufi and founder of the "Illuminationist" school of philosophy.

Solami, Abu 'Abdor-Rahmān (d. 412/1021): One of the great masters of his day, he is the author of *Tabaqāt as-sufiyah* (q.v.).

Tabaqāt as-sufiyah (The Ranks of the Sufis): A classical Arabic work on the lives and sayings of the saints by Solami. Its Persian translation by Ansāri is also a classic.

Tafsir (Commentary on the Koran), entitled Kashf al-asrār (The Unveiling of the Mysteries): A ten volume Persian commentary on the Koran by Maybodi written in the year 520/1126. It deals with each verse from three points of view: linguistic, literal and historical, and Sufi or mystical. Since the author states that he based the work on an earlier work by Ansāri, it is often attributed to the latter author.

Vāseti: See Abu Bakr.

Yahyā ebn Mo'ādh (d. 258/871): A well-known master. KM 122, MSM 179.